Architectural
Study
Drawings

Architectural
Study
Drawings

Daniel M. Herbert

VAN NOSTRAND REINHOLD

VNR _____ New York

Copyright © 1993 by Van Nostrand Reinhold

Library of Congress Catalog Card Number 92-26750
ISBN 0-442-01204-7

Van Nostrand Reinhold is a division of
I(T)P International Thomson Publishing. ITP logo
is a trademark under license.

Printed in the United States of America.

Van Nostrand Reinhold
115 Fifth Avenue
New York, New York 10003

International Thomson Publishing
Berkshire House
168-173 High Holborn
London WC1V 7AA, England

Thomas Nelson Australia
102 Dodds Street
South Melbourne 3205
Victoria, Australia

Nelson Canada
1120 Birchmount Road
Scarborough, Ontario M1K 5G4, Canada

16 15 14 13 12 11 10 9 8 7 6 5 4 3 2 1

Library of Congress Cataloging-in-Publication Data

Herbert, Daniel M.
    Architectural study drawings : their character-
istics and their properties as a graphic medium for
thinking in design / Daniel M. Herbert.
        p.   cm.
    Includes bibliographical references and index.
    ISBN 0-442-01204-7
    1. Architectural drawing.   2. Architectural
design.   I. Title.
NA2705.H46   1993
720′.28′4—dc20   92-26750
                                                     CIP

CONTENTS

ACKNOWLEDGMENTS

With this acknowledgment, I am pleased to thank all those who have contributed to the writing of this book.

I am grateful for help from two institutions. A Design Advancement Grant from the National Endowment for the Arts provided direct and essential financial support for research, travel, and writing. A Planning Grant from the University of Oregon provided indirect aid through the opportunity to discuss many of my ideas with Charles Rusch, James Tanaka and Morton Gernsbacher, Forest Pyle, and Kenneth O'Connell.

Among present and former colleagues in the Department of Architecture at the University of Oregon, I am indebted to Jenny Young and Bobby-Jo Novitski for their interest and constructive comments on early drafts of the work, and to John Reynolds for his encouragement and advice on matters of publication. Special thanks go to Charles Rusch for having helped me begin this project years ago, for contributing some of the key ideas on which the book is based, for his valuable review of early drafts of parts of the work, and, not least, for his continued interest in the outcome.

Special thanks also to Paul Laseau, whose support and recommendations at the right times made all the difference in my progress through the project, and to Cecile Whiting for her review of my translations from French texts. I am also indebted to David Bell, who, as editor of the *Journal of Architectural Education* in 1986, encouraged me to broaden my ideas about diagram as medium to include all study drawings.

I could not have written this book without the cooperation of the architects I interviewed. I would like to thank Joseph Esherick, Peter Eisenman, Helmut Jahn and his associate Keith Palmer, Robert A. M. Stern, and Stanley Tigerman for giving their time to discuss with me the role of study drawings in their work and for their continued cooperation as the project developed. I would also like to thank those on the staff at each architect's office who assisted in setting up the interviews and providing copyright permissions and reproductions.

Other kinds of help came from my family. From my daughters Nan and Lauren I received personal encouragement that I will always treasure. From my son Jim came a remarkable combination of support: the filial backing I was proud to have, the informed discussion of the issues that added so much to my understanding, the technical advice on how to write a book, and the pitiless editing that challenged every fault. And, finally, from my wife Eleanor I received the day-to-day support that makes creating a long work possible; for her years of giving it, I dedicate this book to her.

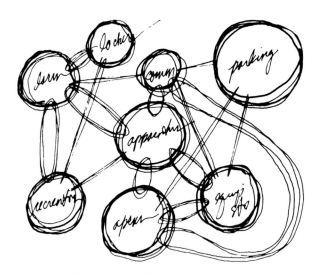

FIGURE Int-1. Edward T. White: rough draft of space adjacency diagram, 1986. *Courtesy Edward T. White.*

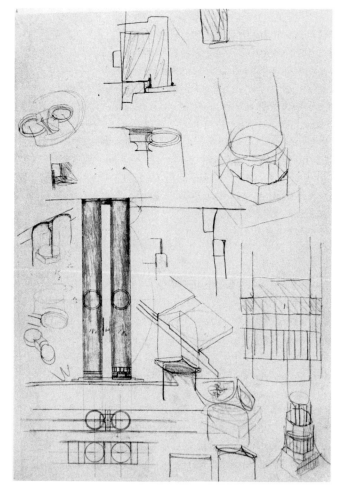

FIGURE Int-2. Carlo Scarpa: study drawing for the Banca Popolare di Verona, Verona, 1973. See figure 7-1 for details about the drawing. *Courtesy Archivio Scarpa.*

Consider the first drawing for an architectural project: say, a rough diagram a designer might make to study the layout of spaces for a recreation building (figure Int-1). Or, later in the working process, a more complex graphic study that mixes freehand and mechanical drawing to explore the development of a pair of interior columns (figure Int-2). These are typical study drawings: the exploratory and developmental sketches architectural designers[1] make in the early phases of design. Even today, when computer-aided systems have taken over many other parts of architectural practice, most designers still make their study drawings by hand in much the same way architects have made them for the past 500 years.

A long tradition is only one reason that study drawings seem to be just a sensible and obvious way to study problems in design. Other reasons—rooted in the architect's training, the nature of human perception and cognition, and a body of cultural assumptions—make it easy for designers in current practice simply to take their study drawings for granted. I will argue in the following chapters, however, that these drawings are more than just a convenient way of working out design problems. They are the designer's principal means of thinking: the origin, nature, and methods of obtaining knowledge in architectural design can be explained largely in terms of a few culture-dependent properties of study drawings.

As instruments of thought, study drawings have a profound influence not only on the early phases of the designer's work, but also on the next phases leading toward construction, and thus on the buildings that are the eventual object of design. For all their importance, however, until recently there has been little basis for understanding either how study drawings work in the design process or how to make them better.

A THEORETICAL STRUCTURE FOR CONSIDERING STUDY DRAWINGS

In the past few years a number of works with an interest in design process drawings have appeared in architec-

INTRODUCTION

[1] I will use the terms *designer* and *architectural designer* interchangeably to refer to those who are involved in design; I will use *architect* as a broader term, since today's architectural practice involves many activities other than design.

tural publications.[2] These works have confirmed the importance of graphics as a field of study, established drawing as a means of graphic thinking, and explored specific techniques for effective drawing in design. I have sought to complement and extend these earlier works by focusing this book on study drawings.

This book is, I believe, the first sustained theoretical treatment of architectural study drawings, and the first to include examples of study drawings from architectural practice as a basis for systematic analysis. The book not only discusses the characteristics of study drawings as a distinct graphic form, but also proposes a theoretical structure of properties for study drawings as a medium for thinking in design. Such a discussion of practical matters and theoretical structure provides a way to understand what designers actually do in their work and how it may be related to research about thinking processes in other disciplines.

CONCEPTS FROM OTHER DISCIPLINES

With appropriate adaptations, certain concepts from other disciplines may be applied to the analysis of study drawings. In the arts and literature, for example, critical analysis typically focuses on interpreting already completed works such as performances, pictures, or written texts—the products of some design or artistic process. In architecture this sort of analysis typically focuses on buildings; that is, on completed design products. Critical analysis is not limited to considering products, however; it can also focus on design processes and their associated graphics, that is, on study drawings. Thus, through adaptation of their application from product to process, the analytic tools and ideas developed in the humanities related to the structure of human knowledge—literature, art, art history, philosophy, and linguistics—become available for the analysis of study drawings.

The structure of human knowledge has been of concern in science as well as the humanities. Findings from investigations in neurobiology and cognitive psychology have proposed new ideas about perception

and its relation to thinking, introducing concepts that have important application to understanding how designers go about their work.

These concepts from disciplines in the humanities and sciences show that any representation is inherently problematic, that any medium introduces substantial new issues into its own discourse, and that all thought is inseparable from its medium of formulation and expression. The medium does not hold the content, as our ordinary terminology suggests; medium and content are fused, or perhaps it may be said that the content is a function of the medium. When applied to design, such ideas raise fundamental questions about graphic media and design content, especially about study drawings as the designer's principal means of thought. It is from pursuing these questions that I derive my central argument.

CENTRAL ARGUMENT

In its briefest form, the argument of this book is that the role of study drawings is one not of passive recording but of active participation in formulating the design. Casting media in the role of active participant questions the conventional assumptions of publications, practice, and teaching in design—assumptions that study media are unproblematic graphic tools, that they act as neutral, transparent ways to represent decisions the designer has reached by separate mental operations. In opposition to this assumption, I will argue that these tools are intrinsically problematic and that, as active participants, study media are neither neutral nor transparent.

Implicit in this argument is that, unlike completed presentation drawings, study drawings are always incomplete and contingent—they are made mark by mark within a design task that evolves in real time, and are always poised between an unresolved past and an unpredictable future. These drawings are significant, then, not as completed objects but as part of a graphic thinking process. Understanding study drawings requires considering how mental and graphic processes interact in the real time of the design task.

These interactive processes may be understood through a series of five epistemological properties of study drawings. First, study drawings embody a preexisting order imposed by the parent culture and by the architectural subculture in which they are embedded;

---

[2]Among these works, such authors as Laseau (1986), McKim (1980), and Lockard (1982) have considered the taxonomy and application of techniques for graphic thinking, and Hewitt (1985) has examined the historical and conceptual aspects of representational forms.

this order tacitly determines, for example, what will count as knowledge, who makes drawings, and what issues the design will include. Second, the drawing's graphic processes provide the means to generate (not just record) information as a designer continuously reinterprets one by one the marks that constitute the drawing. Third, study drawings integrate graphic and cognitive processes and thereby introduce an inescapable uncertainty into the design task. Fourth, study drawings incorporate graphic conventions that impose a certain order on the perception, creation, storage, and retrieval of cognitive images, and allow study drawings to change from the informal, private marks of the designer working alone to progressively more formal, public communication with others. Fifth, study drawings support both continuity and change in a dynamic working process of design through the use of two different types of drawings: context drawings, which hold the evolving design decisions in a putative order, and the ambiguous exploration drawings, which are abstracted from the context drawing and act as graphic probes to investigate selected issues. The ambiguity of the exploration drawings enables a designer to read more out of a drawing than he or she puts into it; in short, to generate new meanings within the design task.

To keep the discussion of this argument from getting hopelessly abstract I have sought to ground it in empirical experience. This is not to say that such experience is a test of the argument; rather, that the argument is a way to organize and thereby understand an otherwise diffuse mass of experience—my own and others'. Since my empirical experience in teaching and practice is limited, as any individual's must be, and since little has been published about how designers actually make study drawings, I sought to broaden the base for this analysis by looking to the work of other architects.

INTERVIEWS AND INTENTIONALITY

I visited five well-known architects to find out how they use study drawings: Joseph Esherick in San Francisco, Robert A.M. Stern and Peter Eisenman in New York, and Stanley Tigerman and Helmut Jahn in Chicago.[3] I selected these architects first for their known interest in graphics, but I also sought variety in geographic distribution, firm sizes, and design approaches.

In addition to tape-recording these five architects' comments about their drawings, I photographed the drawings they talked about—typically 30 to 50 each—as time and field conditions permitted. Some of the illustrations in the book (figures 1-9, 1-19, 4-13, 5-5, and 6-6) are reproduced here from my photographs taken during the visits because the original drawings were misplaced in the architect's files before expert copies could be made.

In arranging for these visits, I asked the architects to select drawings from their recent or current work, particularly sequences of drawings that would show their working process, and I advised them that I would like to focus on drawings rather than on design philosophy.

The interviews and the accompanying photographs provide a valuable look at the role of drawing in the work of contemporary architectural designers. Another source that offers both drawings and comments about them is the Le Corbusier Archive.[4] The records for the chapel of Notre Dame du Haupt at Ronchamp are especially useful not only because the building itself is so well known but also because the documentation for the project includes drawings and writings by Le Corbusier as well as other participants and commentators. Through these drawings and writings, Le Corbusier becomes almost a sixth architect in my series of interviews.

A word about these architects' verbal statements and their drawings. In her book on antifascism in American art, art historian Cecile Whiting says:

> Since American artists . . . often voiced their
> political beliefs and the relationship they
> perceived between such opinions and their art, it
> is tempting to use their words as proof of antifascistic
> intention. . . . In my analysis, I try to let the images
> speak for themselves, although sometimes I do
> rally artists' statements to my cause. At other
> times I demonstrate . . . the contrast between
> stated intent and visual realization. . . . In any
> case, I do not consider that written texts from my
> artists' pens provide a source of "truth" or an
> infallible insight into artistic intention; they stand

---

[3]See the references at the end of this introduction regarding citation from the interviews with these architects.

[4]Le Corbusier. 1982. *The Le Corbusier Archive,* ed. H. Allen Brooks. Vol. 20. New York: The Garland Publishing Co.

as just one indicator of artistic meaning, and as documents they must constantly be weighed against other historical evidence—above all, the artworks themselves. (Whiting 1989, 4)

I have taken much the same approach to my architects' comments: statements made by the five architects during the interviews and Le Corbusier's written statements stand as just one interpretation of the role of drawing in their work. But how can any interpretation other than the architect's be allowed? Here it is necessary to distinguish among several ways of interpreting the drawings.

First, a completed drawing—say, some group of lines that may be taken to represent a solid object or, perhaps, an open space—may be interpreted as an indicator of architectural meaning. Critical analysis from other disciplines, when applied to a completed drawing, suggests that its graphic marks become fair game for any viewer's interpretation, that the drawing's author has no special privilege in determining the "real" meaning any more than does the creator of a written text have final control over how it may be interpreted. Peter Eisenman stated this exactly in our interview as he discussed his completed drawings:

> Everybody is allowed to interpret those things the way they want, probably better than I. I am the worst interpreter of the marks, because I am closest to them. [My interpretation is] more covered with all sorts of unreliable specific aims of mine; I'm going to read this the way I want to read it. It may not be the way I should read it, so I'm the worst interpreter. I wouldn't trust me at all with these marks.

Thus Eisenman says that anyone's interpretation of the completed drawing may be allowed. But this allowance is misleading because it applies only to completed drawings. As the discussion in this book holds, for the incomplete study drawing—that is, the drawing in process—the architectural designer's interpretation is unique: he or she is the only person whose interpretation gets incorporated into the evolving design task and, consequently, into the finished building. If, in the working process, the designer has read certain ambiguous lines as describing a solid object, then that is what they become.

Separate from these issues of the drawing as indicator of meaning is the matter of the drawing as evidence of the designer's working process. Here, because individuals are notoriously unreliable observers of their own actions and intentions, the drawing as artifact is again open to anyone's interpretation. Since any study drawing is made mark by mark in real time, the completed drawing becomes a record of its own process. In analyzing and comparing such records from many sources, I have made inferences beyond statements from the architects' interviews or their writings, and in several cases I have questioned accounts or opinions offered by the architects themselves. The design task is so complex and the role of drawing in it has been so much taken for granted that it should be no surprise to find varying interpretations of the graphic evidence on the page. Getting the graphic evidence required for such a close analysis raises special problems in documenting and reproducing the designer's work.

DOCUMENTATION AND REPRODUCTION OF STUDY DRAWINGS

This book concentrates on the role of drawing in design, with only an occasional mention of the role of models. Designers routinely use study models as well as drawings in contemporary practice. I have omitted the analysis of models from the book, however, because their role is usually secondary to that of drawings, because the documentation of study models is even harder to obtain than that of drawings, and because models present impossible problems in reproduction.

Study drawings present their own problems of documentation and reproduction. A brief discussion of these problems here will help readers understand the role of illustrations in the body of the book.

First are the problems related to size. It is impractical to copy all drawings at full size. Yet knowing how big a drawing is becomes critical to understanding its role in the designer's thinking. Figures 4-1 and 4-6 show the contrast in graphic presence between the reduced image and the full size of the original drawing. The apparent distance of the scaled-down reproduction in figure 4-1—reduced to about 4 percent of its area at full size—makes it a remote object, while the full-size excerpt in figure 4-6, even though it shows just a small part of the original, almost invites a designer to pick up a stick of charcoal and join Le Corbusier in the work. Reproducing the whole sheet of this drawing at full size in the book would require a formidable fold-out page of about 46 by 30 inches.

Another set of problems concerns the drawing's physical form. Study drawings are graphically so informal that even if they are saved by their authors, it is difficult to organize and prepare them for publication. The drawings often lack dates or notes to indicate their relation to one another, and drawings made as overlays on tracing paper do not preserve the essential graphic context of the underlying drawing. Furthermore, the graphic variation and irregularity of many study drawings—often with very light lines and shading and hints of the paper's texture—make exact reproduction difficult even under controlled conditions in a photo lab.

In a few cases I have included reproductions of formal presentation drawings to serve as contrasts to the informal study drawings that preceded them. In general, however, I have avoided including drawings or photographs of the completed buildings that were eventually developed from the study drawings under consideration because that would invite comparisons to see how close the early drawing came to representing, or matching, the eventual building.[5] As the discussion in chapter 7 will show, matching a building is only one aspect of representation. For study drawings, such matching is largely beside the point because the building did not exist when the drawing was made. The purpose of the analysis is not to see whether the early drawing matched the final building but to understand how designers actually make study drawings—to discover the role of these drawings in the design task and its related working process.

DESIGN TASK AND WORKING PROCESS

Two terms used above and in the following chapters—*design task* and *working process*—require explanation here, not because they are unusual in themselves but because they must be distinguished from similar terms commonly used in discussions about design.

I will use the term *design task* rather than the more commonly used *design problem* to avoid the implica-

tion that design involves addressing problems that exist as separate entities, like puzzles that have predetermined correct answers. Thus I define the design task functionally, as the designer's graphic investigations of a set of programmatic requirements, site conditions, and technological considerations. Since these program requirements and related conditions themselves inevitably lack full definition, the design task is one of inquiry, of an evolving search for consequences. Donlyn Lyndon (1982, 6-7) writes that "each move in the tentative evolution of design is predicated on the conditions established by its predecessors. Predicated, that is to say, on an assessment of the work done so far as viewed from the various design domains that the architect has taken to be pertinent. . . ."

The design task is always evolving, then; it is an act of inquiry rather than a fixed assignment. It does not provide an answer, or at least it does not only provide an answer such as a particular structure in a particular place and time. Indeed the current design task may create new design tasks or raise new questions. It may, for example, invoke, transcend, or reject certain historical precedents and thus call for new interpretations of other drawings or completed buildings. Furthermore, the design task creates new knowledge in the same sense that Umberto Eco (1976, 274) has said of art: "Common artistic experience . . . teaches us that art not only elicits feelings but also *produces further knowledge.* The moment that the game of intertwined interpretations gets under way, the text compels one to reconsider the usual codes and their possibilities" (Eco's emphasis). For design, Eco's observation means that the subject matter of the "game" is always open and increasing. Furthermore, for the designer, design is cumulative; the design task of any given project brings new knowledge to every next design task.

Every design task is accomplished through some working process. I will use the term *working process* to refer to the ordinary operational elements of the design task—such as making freehand rather than mechanical drawings in certain situations, or making some kinds of drawings faster than others—elements and operations that are common to most design tasks. Thus I see the working process as a series of concrete operations in relation to the more abstract *design process.* Where discussions of design process in other publications usually concern long-range strategic directions of the design work, discussion of the working process here will refer to short-range tactical steps.

---

[5]In many cases the projects for which the drawings were made will not have been completed at the time of this book's publication.

Individual idiosyncrasies aside, the working process of design involves a dynamic and cyclic mixture of perception, cognition, and action, all involving study drawings and all interacting with a shifting background of cultural assumptions.

FROM THEORY TO APPLICATION

The book's approach through the design task and the working process keeps the theoretical analysis grounded in practical experience. The analysis not only starts from drawings made by real architects on real projects but also returns to those drawings and to the comments made about them in the interviews. This approach, although focused on theoretical analysis, invites readers to find applications to their own work.

These applications may offer readers with an interest in design a basis for making study drawings more effectively in practice, for reexamining the roles of media in architectural education, and for facing new issues in research and development for computer-aided design systems. Readers from other disciplines—scholars in the humanities and sciences who want to understand the role of artifacts such as drawings in generating new knowledge, for example—may be more concerned with the epistemological properties of study drawings. Although my views of the theoretical issues have prompted several applications that make sense to me, I must echo the remark quoted above from the interview with Peter Eisenman and urge that "... everybody is allowed to interpret those things the way they want...." I will propose a few applications, then, noting those related to practice and teaching below and leaving those about computer-aided systems for the appendix.

APPLICATIONS IN PRACTICE

By *practice* I mean making study drawings, whether in the professional office or in the teaching studio. Thus the following applications concern anyone with an interest in the effectiveness of study drawings—students and teachers as well as interns and architects.

An important group of applications has to do with informed choice. With a theoretical basis and comparative examples, designers will have a basis for choosing what role media ought to play in their work. Such choices may influence what media to use, what kinds of drawings to make at various stages of the work, and how to regard analytic procedures in relation to design synthesis drawings. Designers will also have a framework in which to consider how the role of media might change in response to differences in design tasks.

Choices about the role of media may lead to evaluating media products as indicators of working processes. Both professional and student designers will have an opportunity to compare their study drawings and their working processes with those of architects whose finished buildings are widely known. Finding that these prominent architects make study drawings much like those in ordinary practice may give designers more respect for their own drawings and more incentive to save them. Saved drawings—with the aid of a theoretical structure by which to understand them—offer the opportunity to review the sequence of graphic thinking through the course of a project. Such a review could make it possible to identify key decisions, to evaluate drawings by evidence of graphic effectiveness rather than good looks, and to survey the working process for potential improvements.

Readers may infer specific improvements in the working process from material in the last three chapters of the book. From the discussion in chapter 5, designers can understand and then use the differences between incremental refinements and major reorganizations, and from chapter 6 they can obtain some insight into matters of communication within a design working group. Chapter 7 discusses the important distinction between context and exploration drawings, suggests ways to make exploration drawings quickly, makes a case for keeping a fast, steady working pace, and considers issues related to the design workplace.

Beyond the importance of making study drawings more effectively is the possibility of using graphics in new applications. The argument that graphic media are active participants in design thinking is a challenge to designers—a challenge to regard study media as a creative resource. I suggest a few responses to that challenge here only as a means of referring readers to the discussions and illustrations in the text. A seemingly modest but actually powerful step, for example, is to take a free approach to the interpretation of ordinary study drawings by intentionally misreading graphic conventions or acknowledging graphic accidents as a part of the working process. More complex and still more powerful are the possibilities of adopting an explicit graphic strategy for the design task and introducing deliberate devices to extend the design task beyond its built-in uncertainty, as described in chapters 4 and 5.

APPLICATIONS IN TEACHING

Much of the discussion about applications in practice also pertains to teaching: readers will be able to apply many of the ideas from the book in teaching graphics classes and design studios. In the graphics classroom, teachers and students can engage both theoretical and practical issues concerning the role of study media in design. In the design studio, they can apply their theoretical knowledge not only as a skill in making effective study drawings but also as an element of design content. Below I will outline applications along these lines based on my recent teaching experience.

From the premises described in this book I developed an advanced media course combining both the theory and the practice of study drawings. The theoretical part of the course focuses on the epistemological properties of these drawings and provides a theoretical basis for students to understand the generative role of drawing in their work. The practical part of the course uses demonstrations, individual tutorials, and analysis of the students' own drawings to broaden and extend the students' skills in making study drawings. A more extended description of this course is included in the 1991 Education Honors monograph (Herbert 1992).

The premises of this book also provide a basis for application in the design studio. For the past several years I have conducted a one-term design studio that includes study drawings both as a skill and as an element of content. I treat issues of skill by demonstrating how to make context and exploration drawings and by critiquing the form as well as the content of the students' study drawings. Including study drawing as content brings study media out of the background and into the foreground: I expect students to engage study drawings at a level equivalent to that of program, physical and social context, and technology. Bringing study media in as foreground content involves special teaching approaches. I prepare readings and discussions on critical issues and I ask students to date and save study drawings, to combine manipulated photocopy collages with drawing, to adopt an explicit graphic strategy, to cultivate graphic accidents, and to make cross-readings of graphic conventions.

Integrating media as content in the design studio has three effects. First, it raises the level of the students' involvement in the studios and the quality of their work. Second, it generates an unusual interest in design process: most students become aware, for example, that even if they do not adopt a specific graphic strategy, their graphic study media influence the content as well as the form of their design. And third, in the course of the work the students engage many of the central questions of contemporary criticism, not only in design but in other fields: How is representation related to an external reality? Can we *re-present* something that does not yet exist? How can architects deal with uncertainty? What do critical issues in design mean to a building's users and owners? How are graphic and verbal expressions related? Are rules and conventions necessary? How is creativity related to rules?

In contemporary practice some applications of media as content have been employed in a stylistic approach that has been called *deconstruction.* This approach—whatever its value—has thus by association imposed its ideological and stylistic program on these applications. I have found, however, that engaging study media as content does not presuppose any particular style of design. The critical issues of *order, representation, interpretation, uncertainty, self-reference,* and *the role of rules and conventions* cut across stylistic programs. These issues deserve discussion on their own merits because they pose fundamental questions, not only about the role of media, but about every aspect of design.

REFERENCES

Eco, Umberto. 1976. *A Theory of Semiotics.* Bloomington: Indiana University Press.

Herbert, Daniel. 1992. A media course in architectural study drawings. *American Institute of Architects Architectural Education Programs Monograph, 1991 Education Honors.* Pp. 37-42.

Hewitt, Mark A. 1985. Representational forms and modes of conception. *Journal of Architectural Education* 39 (2): 2-9.

Laseau, Paul. 1986. *Graphic Thinking for Architects and Designers.* 2d ed. New York: Van Nostrand Reinhold.

Lockard, William Kirby. 1982. *Design Drawing.* Tucson, Ariz.: Pepper Publishing.

Lyndon, Donald. 1982. Design: inquiry and implication. *Journal of Architectural Education* 25 (3, Spring): 2-8.

McKim, Robert H. 1980. *Thinking Visually.* Belmont, Calif.: Wadsworth, Inc., Lifetime Learning Publications.

Whiting, Cecile. 1989. *Antifascism in American Art.* New Haven, Conn.: Yale University Press.

Special note regarding citations from interviews—the dates and locations of interviews were as follows: Joseph Esherick, September 5, 1989, San Francisco; Robert A.M. Stern, September 7, 1989, New York; Peter Eisenman, September 8, 1989, New York; Stanley Tigerman, September 11, 1989, Chicago; Helmut Jahn, September 12, 1989, Chicago. Throughout the book quotations are taken from my unpublished transcripts of these interviews; in order to avoid repetition, I have not given these quotations individual citations. Quotations from published works by these architects are cited in the normal manner.

I
The Characteristics of
Study Drawings

In his brief analysis of architectural papers Goodman (1968, 218-21) considers three sorts of documents: specifications, renderings, and plans (by *plans* he apparently means construction drawings). *Specifications,* he says, present few problems in that they are written in ordinary language. Architectural renderings are more complex, however: he defines a *rendering* as a sketch, and notes that "[a] sketch does not define a work ... but rather IS one" (p. 193, Goodman's emphasis). Construction drawings are even more complex than renderings, he says, because of their mixture of pictorial representation, words, and numerals. He goes on to observe that the architect's notational language, like a musical score, was developed to allow the participation of many hands, and he concludes (somewhat lamely, I think) that this language is a "mixed and transitional case."

Goodman considered only the most public and most complete of the architect's papers. Had he examined the less public and often incomplete study drawings, he might have thought the whole mix more curious still, for study drawings raise peculiar new concerns. These new concerns—both practical and theoretical—form the basis for the following discussion. I will set theoretical concerns aside for later chapters, however, and first consider several practical matters, beginning with the study drawing's relation to the rest of the work—especially their relation to other sorts of drawings.

RELATION TO OTHER DRAWINGS

Despite their importance in the early phases of design, study drawings constitute just a fraction of the architect's duties. Perhaps as little as 10 to 15 percent of an architectural firm's total hours on a typical project are allocated to conceiving and developing the building's design—that is, to making study drawings. The balance of the architectural work includes providing various technical and support services and making the public kinds of drawings Goodman brought up—the formally rendered presentation drawings, and the technically detailed construction drawings.

Unlike the outward-looking public drawings, study drawings have a private, inward focus. Typically, an individual designer uses study drawings to conduct an internal graphic dialogue about the design issues at hand. Or, on sizeable projects, several designers may coordinate their work within a (usually small) working

1
PRACTICAL MATTERS

The architect's papers are a curious mixture.

NELSON GOODMAN, *Languages of Art*

group by means of study drawings. The inward focus of study drawings implies a private, or perhaps semi-private, audience of insiders, compared with the public audience outside the working group. Addressing the public audience for a project is the purpose of presentation and construction drawings. Presentation drawings, for example, tell an architect's client how spaces will be related within the building and what it will look like, and construction drawings provide technical information for material suppliers and construction crews. Study drawings almost never serve such formal and public purposes.

The inward focus of study drawings accounts for their characteristic rough appearance. Graphic conventions are simplified: although designers usually construct even their private study drawings as plan, section, elevation, or perspective views, they often ignore these conventions' finer points. Because the designer is address-

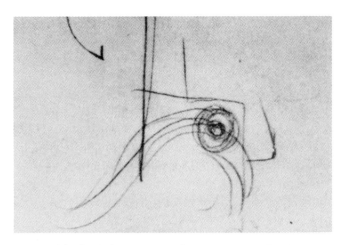

FIGURE 1-2. Carlo Scarpa: part of a study drawing for the Gallerie dell'Accademia museum installation, 1949. See figure 7-9 for the whole drawing. *Courtesy Archivio Scarpa.*

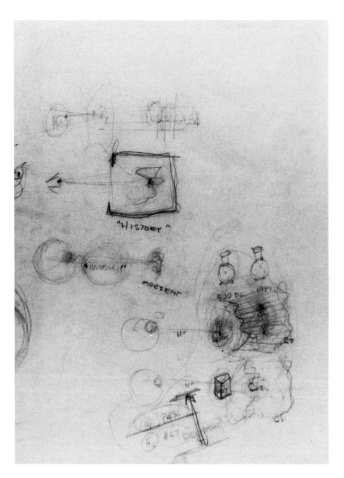

FIGURE 1-1. Author: part of a page of graphic notes from a desk critique with student concerning the role of history in design project, October 1987. Light pencil on lightweight tracing paper; 14″ × 10″ (from a 27″ × 10″ original). *Courtesy Daniel Herbert.*

ing a limited, internal audience, study drawings sometimes contain idiosyncratic notations made up on the spot (figure 1-1); public drawings, aimed at an external and often anonymous audience, necessarily rely on a widely shared system of conventions and symbols for communication. And while presentation drawings preserve conventional scale relations and spatial illusion, study drawings often neglect both scale and illusion by disregarding customary scales, by showing only rough proportions, by representing fragments of buildings, or by expressing purely abstract qualities of a design idea (figure 1-2). Since study drawings are intended for a private audience, designers often draw them in loose formats, on thin sketchpaper, at the margins of larger drawings, or on scraps of paper, envelopes, or whatever is at hand (figures 1-3, 1-4). Such informalities again set study drawings apart from the more formal presentation and construction drawings, which are literally published and serve as parts of formal legal contracts.

Furthermore, study drawings differ from other drawings in their timing: the bulk of architectural study drawings are made during the early conceptual and developmental phases of the work. A designer may make hundreds of study drawings over a period of months before starting presentation drawings at the end of conceptual development. Study drawings are not altogether confined to early conceptual phases, however; on any project, further study drawings may be needed in later phases of the work—to sketch out a solution to a detail problem that comes up during the preparation of construction drawings or during construction, for example.

Finally, in comparison to other forms of drawing, study drawings lack a strong theoretical basis. The graphic theory for making public presentation drawings and construction drawings is well understood and its application has been codified through teaching and practice into rules on which anyone can rely to get good results (figure 1-5). But until recently publications about graphics in design have given little attention to establishing a theoretical basis for private drawings. Consequently, architectural designers still use study drawings mostly by custom, without an adequate understanding of their essential role in our thinking about design.

Such contrasts in audience, timing, convention, and theoretical basis seem to suggest that study drawings are the antithesis of presentation and construction drawings. This view of the differences between study drawings and other architectural drawings is both too polarized and too narrow, however; a broader view is needed to describe the relation of study drawings to

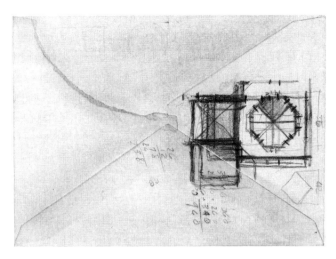

FIGURE 1-4. Author: study drawing for design competition, 1982. Colored pencil on white envelope; 7″ × 5″. *Courtesy Daniel Herbert.*

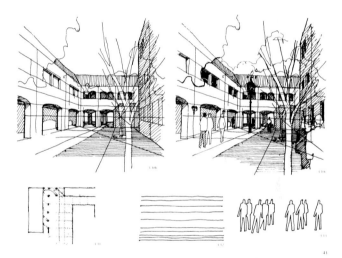

FIGURE 1-5. Paul Laseau: example of steps in constructing a perspective drawing. *Courtesy Paul Laseau.*

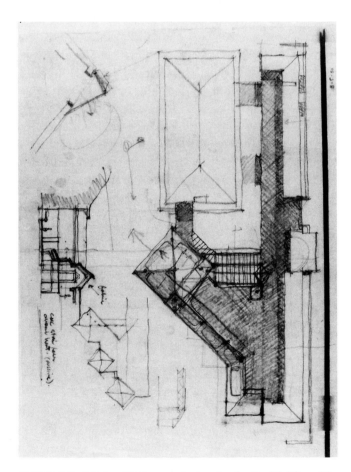

FIGURE 1-3. Michael Keller: study drawing for the McMinnville Public Library, McMinnville, Oregon, 1980. Ink, black and colored pencil on lightweight tracing paper; 13″ × 10″. *Courtesy Michael Keller.*

each other and to other architectural drawings (figure 1-6). Study drawings are not all of one kind: they may be either more or less abstract or they may progressively change from private to public. As the following chapters will discuss in detail, the degree of abstraction needed varies according to the circumstances of the design task. The transformation from private to public is a routine part of any project's development, however: designers normally make their private study drawings according to the same graphic conventions that are used in public drawings so that the information in study drawings can be incorporated directly into subsequent work.

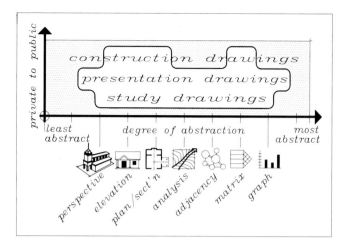

FIGURE 1-6. Relation of study drawings to other kinds of architectural drawings. *Courtesy Daniel Herbert.*

MAKING STUDY DRAWINGS

Recognizing the role of study drawings in relation to other kinds of architectural work helps to explain some of the designer's graphic choices. For example, the short and intense time allowed for study drawings means that most of these drawings must be done quickly: precise and meticulous drawings are too rigid and time-consuming to carry through the whole design task. What designers need for conceptual investigation are swift and free-flowing graphic instruments that can match the pace of their thinking—expressive freehand lines with the immediacy of a gesture (figure 1-7), slashing lines along a straightedge (figure 1-8), or quick lines that can catch a fleeting idea in a few seconds (figure 1-9). From time to time the designer also needs carefully scaled drawings made to confirm decisions made by the rough freehand sketches and to provide a basis for a new round of investigations. These scaled drawings typically are made by the designer's technical assistants, such as those made by Maisonnier for Le Corbusier's chapel at Ronchamp (figure 1-10). Yet even such obviously slow drawings retain the inward direction characteristic of study drawings, evident in the uncomposed placement of the individual drawings on the page and their lack of graphic flair that would keep them from attracting and holding the attention of a non-technical public audience. Their inward purpose also shows in the drawings' lack of notes, dimensions, and cross references, which would prevent their use as technical documents for construction.

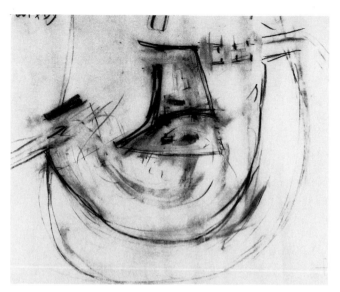

FIGURE 1-7. Le Corbusier: part of a sketch site plan for the chapel at Ronchamp; June 6, 1950; see figure 4-1 for the complete drawing. Charcoal on heavy tracing paper. © *1922 ARS, N.Y./SPADEM, Paris.*

The role of study drawings offers further graphic choices. An absence of formal requirements means that designers have considerable latitude (subject, perhaps, to an architectural firm's policies) about the graphic quality of their study drawings, and what media to use. This room for choice accounts for stylistic variations in drawing; although the graphic character of presentation and construction drawings looks generally similar from one architectural firm to another, designers' study drawings have markedly personal drawing styles.

The intensity of Helmut Jahn's study drawings is instantly recognizable, for example. In part, Jahn's remarks in the interview about his study drawings explained this intensity as he commented on the distinction between study drawings and presentation drawings (figures 1-11, 1-12):

Sometimes . . . the drawings you do in a great deal of stress, and quick, sometimes they're actually the best drawings, the ones you do with a lot of agony. When you want to make a drawing, that's the worst time; when people ask me to make a sketch for the rental brochure, two years later, after the building is designed, then I get really mad, because I don't feel I draw to make nice drawings.

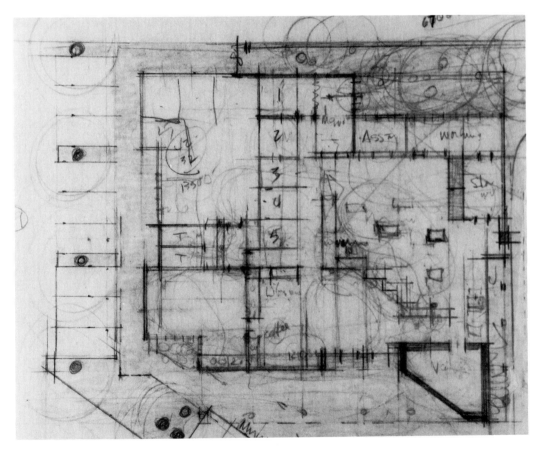

FIGURE 1-8. (Top) Carlo Scarpa: part of Figure Int-2. (Bottom) Author: part of study drawing for commercial building, Eugene, Oregon, 1968. Pencil on medium-weight tracing paper; 9½″ × 8½″. (Top) *Courtesy Archivio Scarpa;* (Bottom) *Courtesy Daniel Herbert.*

FIGURE 1-9. Robert Stern: study drawings for U.S. Embassy annex, Budapest, Hungary, 1989. Soft pencil on lightweight tracing paper; 13″ × 11″. *Courtesy Robert A.M. Stern Architects.*

I don't like to do drawing when I have to make a drawing; somebody says "Can you do a nice elevation?" I don't like to do that. It's not that I can't do that. The drawings are very different.

A lot of these drawings we use in presentations—the funny thing is, sometimes the sketches show more than the finished perspective.

Elsewhere in the interview, Jahn established that he uses his study drawings also for communication about design issues to his staff: "Sometimes the second-, third-generation drawings, they're only made because somebody else did another drawing after I made the initial sketch." Robert Stern's comment suggested agreement about the use of study drawings within the design group: "I suppose one is interested in drawings because of the dialogue that I think is uniquely fascinating about architecture." And, according to Joseph Esherick, the study drawings he makes in working meetings with

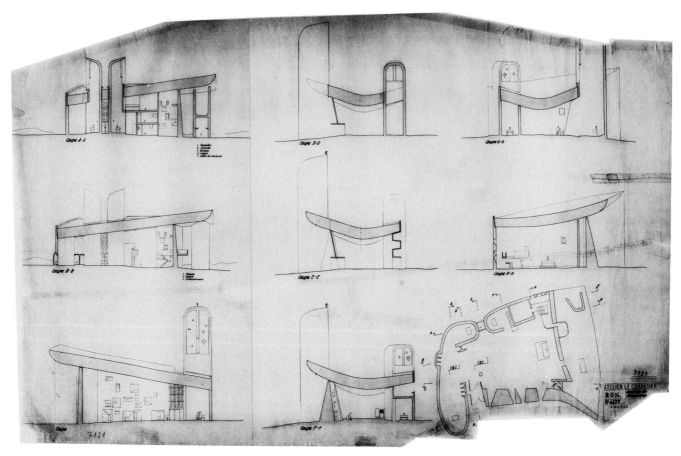

FIGURE 1-10. Le Corbusier: sections through the chapel at Ronchamp drawn by Maisonnier, 195?. Ink on heavy tracing paper; 1390mm × 900mm (about 55″ × 35″). © *1922 ARS, N.Y./SPADEM, Paris.*

residential clients (figure 1-13) have the same investigative purpose, unlike presentation drawings:

> One of the interesting byproducts of this approach is that we very rarely do fancy rendered elevations or perspectives—presentation drawings—when we're working this way. There are a number of houses that we've done where the client has never seen a complete elevation.

These statements underline the role of study drawings as private, investigative instruments. Any other use is incidental.

Incidental uses of study drawings are not uncommon, however. Making study drawings in working meetings with clients is frequent in current practice, usually in the design of single-family residences—as in Esherick's account—rather than for larger projects. Other breaks in the barrier between private and public drawings occur when architects discuss their study drawings in

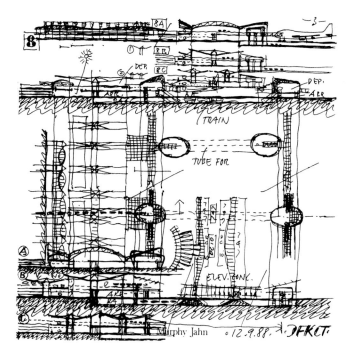

FIGURE 1-11. Helmut Jahn: study drawing for American Airlines terminal, John F. Kennedy Airport, New York, 1988. Ink on bond paper; 8½″ × 8½″. *Courtesy Helmut Jahn.*

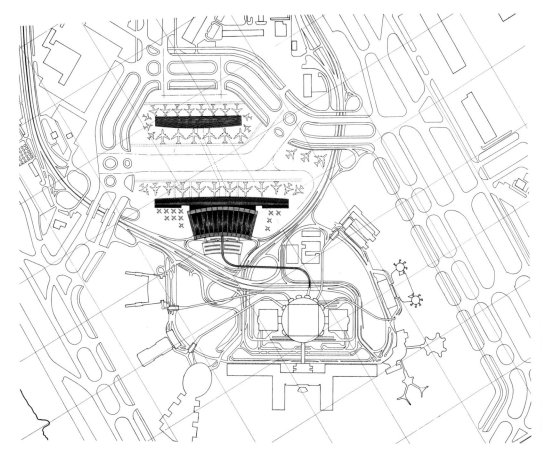

FIGURE 1-12. Murphy/Jahn, Architects: presentation drawing for American Airlines Terminal, John F. Kennedy Airport, New York, 1989. One of several plan, elevation, section, and perspective drawings made by the firm's technical staff. *Courtesy Helmut Jahn.*

FIGURE 1-13. Joseph Esherick: study drawing elevation for house, San Francisco, 1986. Pencil on lightweight tracing paper; part of 25″ × 12″. *Courtesy Joseph Esherick.*

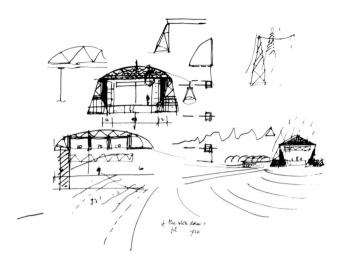

FIGURE 1-14. Gerald McDonnell: study drawings for a park pavilion, Eugene, Oregon, 1991. Ink on medium-weight tracing paper; part of 25″ × 12″. *Courtesy Gerald McDonnell, Architect.*

interim conferences with clients or include them as supplements to more formal presentations (figure 1-14). Thus, although the barrier between private and public drawings is not absolute, study drawings are distinguishable from other architectural drawings by their combined instrumental purpose and informal character.

Architects sometimes make these informal drawings in equally informal circumstances: Jahn spoke of drawing at a ski lodge and on a pool deck, Robert Stern of jotting down drawings on the back of appointment cards while on a plane, Peter Eisenman of drawing in his garden at Princeton, and Stanley Tigerman of drawing anywhere with anything. Perhaps Tigerman's comment best sums up the spontaneous yet purposeful spirit of the study drawing: "This is a drawing on the back of a place mat (figure 1-15). You can draw if you have an instrument; if you don't you can just take a knife and get some blood. . . . [It doesn't matter] where you draw."[1]

Architectural designers at work produce so many study drawings that the sheer quantity of them raises another practical matter: what to do with completed study drawings?

---

[1]Although the place mat Tigerman referred to was saved as part of the project file, there is some doubt about its author. Tigerman remembers the lunch meeting, but he is unclear about whether he or one of his associates made the drawing.

SAVING STUDY DRAWINGS

Since study drawings are by definition exploratory and developmental, any drawing is rendered obsolete almost instantly by a next drawing. Furthermore, the whole sequence of study drawings from early conception through development is superseded by the presentation and construction drawings that always follow. While presentation drawings and construction documents are—not least for legal reasons—virtually always preserved, study drawings may be treated differently because of their quantity, their informality, their obsolescence, and the expense of handling and storing them.

The drawings for even a modest-sized project, such as Stern's U.S. Embassy annex in Budapest, serve to illustrate the practical problems involved in saving drawings. At the time of the interview, the file of saved drawings for the project contained about 50 drawing sheets, such as the one shown in figure 1-9, for the two-to-three-month schematic phase of the work. This file did not include drawings by any of the firm's technical staff, only selections from Stern's own drawings. Of these drawings, Stern said: "For each one here there are ten or fifteen more that I tossed away. I probably save too much . . . but it would be endless, endless." The saved drawings were typically informal, with irregular sizes and shapes, different marking media and papers; some but not all were dated. Although he had done the drawings about four months before and many of the

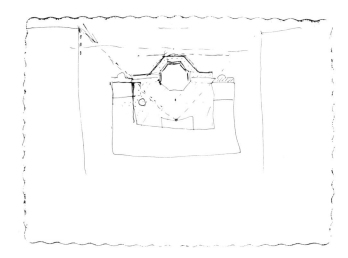

FIGURE 1-15. Stanley Tigerman: sketch for house, Palm Beach, Florida, 1986. Ink on back of paper place mat; 14″ × 10″. *Courtesy Tigerman McCurry Architects.*

days ago, you're really screwing it up. But once the project is finished, these things are in the archive and that's where they belong, period. Once in a while I have been asked to document a project for an exhibition or something like that.

So even in their principal instrumental role these drawings have a short life—perhaps a few days, but usually only hours or minutes—serving mainly as a basis for some next drawing that renders it obsolete. Why save study drawings at all, then? Stern's answer was this:

> The history books, historians, . . . so we can have this meeting. I've written an introduction to a book about architectural drawings, *The Architect's Eye,* and I have been trained as an historian as well as an architect, so I know what the value of saving things is. I had a sense of my own destiny and that's why I save them.

> There are other ones in which the design idea of the building has achieved a certain stated worthiness, a design idea someone might really be interested in the meaning of. . . . But I think that some of my drawings are interesting as drawings and they are definitely interesting as we'd like to know how people develop. . . . I think I've become full grown, I have . . . [attained] . . . a kind of stumbling process. How things happen, people are always interested in how things happen; I am and I know other people are. So that's why the drawings are interesting.

Eisenman, on the other hand, has a special reason for saving drawings, as this excerpt from the interview with him explains:

> **DH:** Does [the drawing] have any purpose beyond just being there?

> **PE:** As you know, as an architect I'm very interested in process, the process of drawing. To me the process has as much importance as the work itself. So I'm obviously trying to keep the documentation because it's important to me. Whenever I publish something I usually publish with documentation, as you saw in the house of cards, so a lot of that is really important.

drawings would be unintelligible to others as works on their own, Stern could recall the purpose and circumstances of each drawing in detail. As to the drawings' obsolescence, all the drawings in the file were typical of study drawings in that they had been superseded by later study drawings or by presentation drawings. Asked if he ever referred to a saved drawing, Stern said:

> No, . . . once I've done it, no. In the terms of the project, five days later, I might go back and say we've gotten lost somewhere, we should find that drawing I did about five days ago; it seemed to be better. But . . . the other way around is that the project architect who is working with me will come back to me and say it looked a lot better five

DH: Do you ever refer back to a drawing from another project?

PE: Oh yes, they have a processural [*sic*] importance, yes, very definitely.

Eisenman selects some drawings over others, however; when asked if he saved all his drawings, he said: "I guess so; not the sketches I make out in the drafting room, when we're working, just doodling around, but I mean all the conceptual drawings, I think I keep." Eisenman saved all of his conceptual sketches for the Columbus Convention Center project (figure 1-16).

Jahn saves still more: he makes his drawings on full-, half-, or quarter-size pieces of 8½-by-11-inch bond paper, each sheet dated (with rare exceptions, as in figure 1-17) and, if sheets are in particular sequence, numbered (figure 1-18). All drawings are saved in albums; their modular size allows their mounting on 11-by-17-inch album pages protected by acetate sleeves, 100 to 200 individual drawings per album. More than a hundred of these albums are stored in sidefile cabinets, indexed chronologically by project. According to Jahn's associate, images of the drawings are also stored and indexed in Jahn's memory so that he can recall the content of any of these drawings and find it almost immediately.

Tigerman saves everything, even transitory overlays that seem obviously incomplete (figure 1-19):

DH: Now, you save all these [other] drawings because they're in the sketchbook; do you also save all the hardline drawings and all the modifying drawings?

ST: All the crude—everything. [The staff are] instructed to save everything, whether they do [pause]. . . . I think they save more or less everything.

DH: So your staff people also save their own drawings?

ST: Every drawing—their drawings, my drawings. At the end of a project—five years after the end of a project, three years—it goes to the warehouse. . . . Sometimes it's identified and sometimes it's not, although I'm pretty careful about that, because we publish a lot of our work and I'm very careful about crediting what people have done.

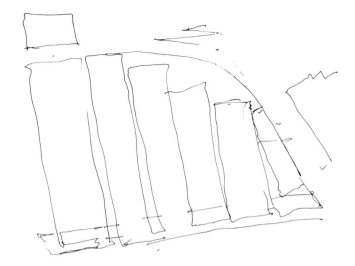

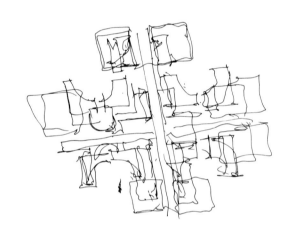

FIGURE 1-16. Peter Eisenman: conceptual sketches for Columbus Convention Center, Columbus, Ohio, 1988. Two out of a group of 13 such sketches, each describing a separate conceptual alternative on a separate drawing page. Ink on heavy white tracing paper from a bound pad; 8½″ × 11″. *Courtesy Peter Eisenman.*

It is not surprising to find that the architects I interviewed have a particular interest in drawing and have saved many of their study drawings; besides my having decided to interview them partly for these reasons, they judge that their prominence gives their work a certain historic regard.

Yet the level of attention these architects give to study drawings is unusual within general architectural practice; although most architectural firms routinely save their presentation drawings and construction documents in some kind of archive, they keep only a few selected study drawings to serve as examples of a project's conceptual exploration and development. Because

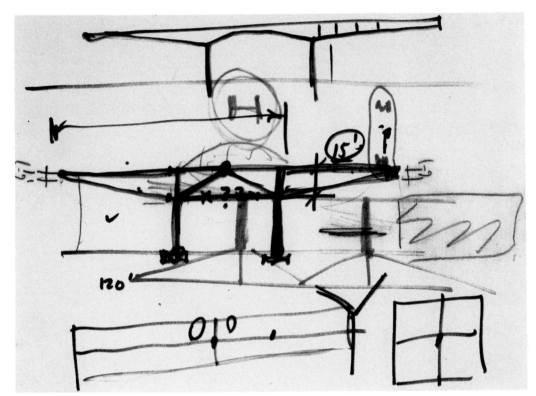

FIGURE 1-17. Helmut Jahn: early sketch for American Airlines terminal, John F. Kennedy Airport, New York (undated; probably August 1988). Red marking pen on bond paper; 11″ × 8½″. *Courtesy Helmut Jahn.*

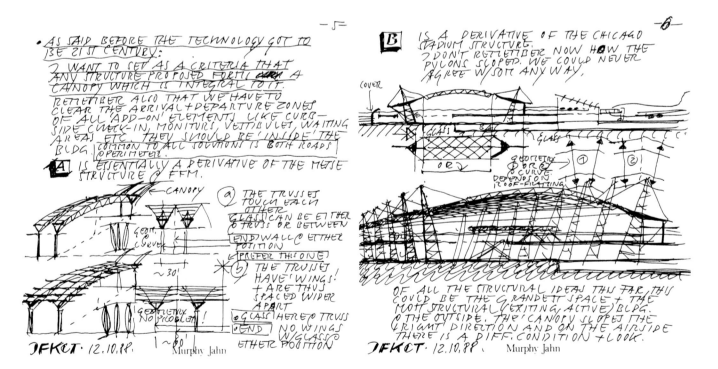

FIGURE 1-18. Helmut Jahn: schematic study drawings for the American Airlines terminal, John F. Kennedy Airport, New York. Two out of a developmental sequence of 14 drawings done over a two-day period. The two drawing pages dated (*12/10/88*, at the lower left) and numbered (*5, 6*, at the upper right) are mounted together on one album page. Ink on bond paper; 8½″ × 8½″. *Courtesy Helmut Jahn.*

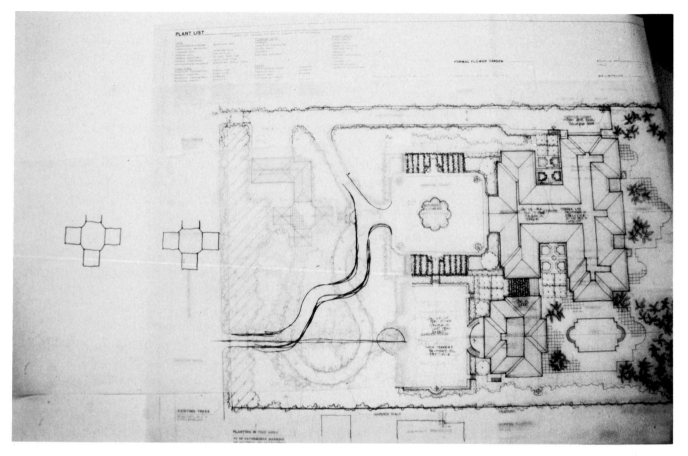

FIGURE 1-19. Stanley Tigerman: overlay study of driveway for house, Palm Beach, Florida, 1989. Tracing paper overlay on a landscape consultant's print. The overlay shows a study for revising the driveway (center) and two studies for revising or relocating the garden pavilion (left); the two drawings for the pavilion are shown displaced from wherever they were drawn originally. Pencil on lightweight tracing paper; 12″ high. *Courtesy Tigerman McCurry Architects.*

study drawings seem so quickly made, so graphically casual, so immediately obsolete, and because indexing and storing them is so difficult and expensive, most of them are trashed in periodic drafting room cleanups.

Such trashing is not unreasonable in itself, but it can lead to mistaken judgments about the role of study drawings in that the drawings that are saved do not represent the whole graphic process. Typically, drawings that are graphically most "presentable" are good candidates for preservation by their author, as are the key drawings along the line of development that led to a project's final form. Study drawings that are published are still less representative because drawings considered for publication always undergo further selection for graphic respectability.

A selection process that eliminates the graphic experiments that failed, the awkward and unpolished drawings made "when we're working, just doodling around," in Eisenman's phrase, means that such drawings are absent from discussions and publications about design. The absence of these drawings provides an unrealistic, fragmented view of the role of graphics in the designer's working process. It suggests that the working process is a straightforward development from stated premises rather than the "stumbling process" Stern described, and it implies that the ordinary drawings designers make day by day are less respectable than they ought to be. The evidence above and in the following chapters suggests, however, that even experienced designers find their way, often haltingly, through the design task largely by means of drawings so ordinary as to be all but unnoticed.

ORDINARY DRAWINGS

In practice, it is curious to see how plain most study drawings are, how similar from one designer to another, and how much the drawings by the prominent architects discussed here are like any of the everyday drawings to be found in a typical office or school studio. It appears that architectural designers from Le Corbusier to Eisenman draw the same kinds of things: schematic plans and variations, fragments of elevations or perspectives, hypothetical details, experimental sections, adjustments to previous decisions, abstract spatial diagrams; all draw with the same familiar graphic conventions and draw in about the same unpretentious fashion. The differences among designers' drawings, including Jahn's remarkably disciplined and prolific drawings, are idiosyncrasies of personal graphic style and variations in subject matter rather than signs of disparate graphic traditions (even Jahn's drawings are sometimes graphically casual—see figure 1-17). The similarities of their drawings suggest that designers approach study drawings from a common background of education and experience, and that they make this kind of drawing mostly by habit, intuition, and circumstance. Designers in architectural practice take for granted the informal role of study drawings just as they do the informal role of language in drafting room discussions about design issues.

In general, study drawings are also taken for granted by architectural educators. Instruction in design media emphasizes the skills essential for effective graphic communication, such as graphic conventions, rendering, and presentation techniques; instruction in study drawings or other process media is treated peripherally, if at all. The lack of explicit and systematic instruction for study drawings means that students and interns must absorb techniques for making these drawings largely by example and inference. They must imitate their mentors while asking themselves these questions: What kinds of drawings should I make to explore design issues? How big should this drawing be? Should lines be straight? What do I draw first, what next? Where should I draw it and how should I talk about it? Which lines should I consider fixed and which mutable? What pace of the work is appropriate; when is it time to change from one kind of drawing to another? How far is personal idiosyncrasy in graphics allowed to go? Which drawings are to be saved and presented, which thrown away? Unspoken questions like these and their unspoken answers form a tacit background to the explicit foreground issues of design content and presentation techniques.

Learning about study drawings in this way—by imitation and inference—may not be efficient, but it is effective: students and interns do absorb study drawing techniques by these means. They learn the informal graphic language and customs and they absorb the graphic habits and attitudes that contribute to making them members of an architectural subculture. And in their turn they continue to use study drawings just as they learned them, as part of a taken-for-granted background for the foreground issues of design.

Such a tacit background is essential, in Goodman's phrase, to allow the participation of many hands. Designers must be able to assume that "lines mean edges," for example, and know that others throughout the architectural profession and the loosely organized construction industry will make the same assumption. These shared assumptions are necessary so that everybody can keep on with the work.

The architectural designer's part of this work has been to explore and develop design ideas by means of study drawings—a role of drawing in design that seems natural, even obvious, in current practice. Yet, as the next chapter will show, it is not the only possible relation between drawing and design.

REFERENCE

Goodman, Nelson. 1968. *Languages of Art*. New York: Bobbs-Merrill Company, Inc.

Ernst Gombrich might have written his description of the postmedieval artist (Gombrich 1960, 173) deliberately to explain the empirical process of architectural design today—the use of a design schema as a starting point for corrections, adjustments, and adaptations that probe the reality of program and site and wrestle with their particulars. His description appears even to include details of the designer's working process—the many study drawings that precede the finished work, the need for constant alertness, the readiness to learn, and the demand to make and remake by means of drawing. This empirical process seems to offer such an obvious, straightforward way of approaching design that contemporary designers will probably not be surprised to find its parallels in the history of other arts.

Gombrich does more than describe the approach of the postmedieval artist, however; he argues that this empirical approach embodied a marked change from that of the Middle Ages. And, although it may come as more of a surprise, this point, too, fits the case of architectural drawings. It was not just a change in design products—that is, the buildings of the time—that characterized the beginning of the Renaissance; it was a change in design processes. New processes, fundamentally different from those of medieval architects, were developed by the artist-architects who worked about 1500 A.D. in central and northern Italy. They defined the empirical role of media in design for the next five centuries, including the way that most designers use media today.

Apparently the role of media in design is not fixed, then; if it has changed before, it may change again. Indeed, an assortment of evidence from many sources suggests the probability of a fundamental change in today's design media. Direct evidence of such change comes, of course, from the steadily increasing use of computer graphics in architectural education and practice. Indirect evidence comes from the radical transitions in current architectural design, from the findings of contemporary critical analysis, and from the transformations of media in other disciplines. Still further evidence, both direct and indirect, comes from the statements about study drawings made by the architects interviewed for this book. Analyzing this assortment of evidence of potential change will be the task of the following discussion.

An example—prompted by Gombrich's observation about art—is available to guide the analysis: the transition in the role of drawing from medieval to Renais-

2
CHANGES IN THE ROLE OF DRAWING IN DESIGN

To the Middle Ages the schema is the image; to the postmedieval artist, it is the starting point for corrections, adjustments, adaptations, the means to probe reality and to wrestle with the particular. The hallmark of the medieval artist is the firm line that testifies to the mastery of his craft. That of the postmedieval artist is not facility, which he avoids, but constant alertness. Its symptom is the sketch, or rather the many sketches which precede his finished work and, for all the skill of hand and eye that marks the master, a constant readiness to learn, to make and match and remake. . . .

E. H. GOMBRICH, *Art and Illusion*

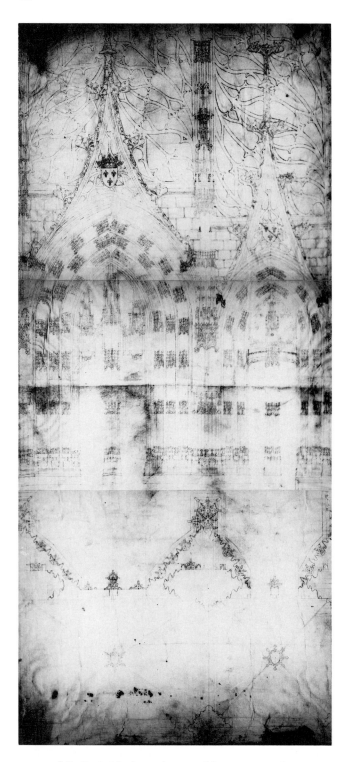

FIGURE 2-1. Probably drawn by one of four masters who were asked to submit a design and cost estimate for completing the west front of the cathedral; Clermont-Ferrand Cathedral, Clermont-Ferrand, France, about 1496. Ink on parchment; 680mm × 1400mm (about 27″ × 55″). The scale is about 1/30, or 3/8″ = 1′0″. *Courtesy of Archives Departementales du Puy-de-Dome.*

sance design. Tracing the history of this previous transition may make it possible to understand and even to influence the direction of potential changes in the role of today's design media.[1] I will start the analysis with a description of the role of drawing in medieval design.

THE ROLE OF DRAWING IN MEDIEVAL DESIGN

During the past three decades, scholars in medieval architecture have brought forward new and more detailed information about late Gothic architects and their design processes. John Harvey, for example, in his book on the medieval architects refutes earlier notions that these architects were either anonymous masons working on the scaffold or clerics who practiced design as a sideline (Harvey 1972). Harvey insists that medieval architects functioned as full-time and highly skilled directors of construction, specially trained, well respected, and often celebrated for their work. He notes that medieval architects were trained from within the building crafts, usually in masonry or carpentry. He describes their early education in book learning, their years of craft apprenticeship, and their final four years of specialized training in drawing. In these final years "[their] main concern was to master and to memorize the very many problems in practical geometry involved in setting-out arch and vault voussoirs, tracery, and proportional design" (99). For medieval architects, training in proportional design consisted of solving, by means of rule and compass, specific geometric layout problems learned by rote and passed down from generation to generation (98). Harvey also comments on the increase in the sophistication of architectural drawings as well as the frequency of their use from the twelfth through the fifteenth centuries, and on into the sixteenth century in northern Europe.

Enough of these drawings by medieval architects still exist to provide a good idea of the role of drawing in design before the sixteenth century. Examples like that of the drawing of the west front of the Clermont-Ferrand Cathedral (figure 2-1) illustrate the remarkable drawing skills of late medieval architects; according to Michael

[1]My focus on the beginning and the end of our graphic tradition does not mean that nothing of interest happened in between. In this chapter I intend to highlight the points at which fundamental shifts occurred—the changes from one cultural schema to another—not to provide a general history of graphics in design.

Davis (1983, 79), this drawing "fulfilled a dual role as a working drawing and as a 'show plan' or impressive elevation." Besides its combination of plan section and elevation, the drawing includes a perspective effect to add a sense of depth. Other drawings having to do directly with laying out the work were often contained within the building itself—incised on the floor of the ambulatory at Clermont-Ferrand (figure 2-2), or on the floors of special drawing lofts, as at Well Cathedral (figure 2-3). François Bucher refers to his having studied more than 2200 medieval plans and designs that were preserved throughout Europe (Bucher 1968, 49). From these studies he lists five kinds of drawings (aside from templates and models), embracing theoretical designs, educational plans, working plans, special plans, and sketch and lodge-books. He notes that Gothic planning "down to the details was based on a highly coordinated system of geometric progression" (50). Bucher gives particular attention to a sketch plan, made about 1500 by Benedikt Ried, for the vaulting over a palace stairway (figure 2-4), describing it as a "quick first concept . . . dashed off entirely with a compass. . . . [Its] quick, almost sloppy design . . . betrays the eye of a master . . ." (56). Bucher's other examples, descriptions, and discussion—including his analysis of drawings from Villard de Honnecourt's sketchbook—emphasize the rule-bound mechanical construction of all these drawings, their reliance on practical (rather than theoretical) geometric precepts, and their use of primary tools such as the straightedge, square, compass, and dividers.

Thus it appears that the medieval architects' drawings consisted largely of geometric layouts derived from and functioning directly within the construction process or even within the building itself. Even the occasional sketch such as that for the Rider Stair shows drawings centered on practical geometry. Citing the geometric basis of these drawings does not suggest that their authors had only a naive or rudimentary understanding of design—rather, the complexity and sophistication of their processes and products argue that the medieval architects were at least as skillful at their work as today's architects are at theirs.

And just as today's architects do, the medieval architects had to learn the graphic language and customs that made them members of the architectural subculture of their own time; they had to acquire its taken-for-granted, tacit background for design. Michel Foucault describes such a cultural (and subcultural) background as a "hidden network" of codes:

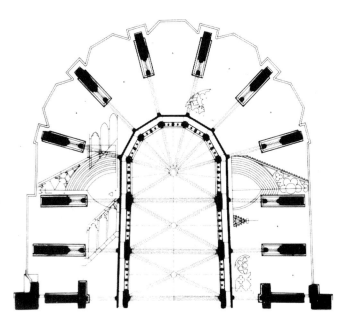

FIGURE 2-2. Drawing of full-sized layout diagrams incised in the stone of the floor at Clermont-Ferrand Cathedral, Clermont-Ferrand, France, thirteenth century. The incised lines are now filled with white mortar to contrast with the dark stone of the floor. *Courtesy of Clermont Cathedral.*

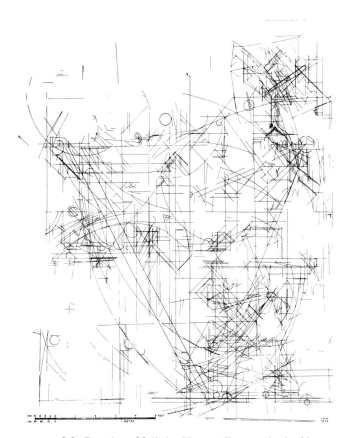

FIGURE 2-3. Drawing of full-sized layout diagrams incised in a plaster "drawing floor" at Wells Cathedral, Wells, England, about 1200. *Copyright drawing by John H. Harvey; reproduced by courtesy of the Royal Archeological Institute.*

The fundamental codes of a culture—those governing its language, its schemas of perception, its exchanges, its techniques, its values, the hierarchy of its practices—establish for every man, from the very first, the empirical orders with which he will be dealing, and within which he will be at home. (Foucault 1970, xx)

For artists and architects at any time, then, the spatial and graphic aspects of these fundamental codes establish the empirical orders with which they will be dealing, and within which they will be at home in their own disciplines. For the medieval architect, the fundamental codes determined that the conceptual content—the meaning—of design drawings was governed by established rules for their interpretation as well as their construction. Lacking the years of medieval craft training, the years of practical geometry that informed these drawings, and the fixed codes that determined their meaning, today's designers and scholars cannot interpret these medieval drawings as their makers did. Before 1500 A.D. drawing for construction and drawing for design coincided in ways that are inconceivable today.

THE ROLE OF DRAWING IN RENAISSANCE DESIGN

Around 1500, however, the role of drawing in design shifted. After 1500, the fundamental codes for design drawings and construction drawing no longer coincided. While masons and carpenters no doubt continued to make geometric layout drawings, a new sort of drawing—the study drawing—was invented in art and architecture. That the invention of study drawings occurred in these two fields at the same time was no accident because it involved the same individuals. Mark Hewitt, in his article entitled "Representational Forms and Modes of Conception," describes the role of these artist-architects in developing the new form of drawing in design:

> Renaissance artist/architects, Leonardo foremost, gave us the skeptical, modern, trial-and-error mode of design, stemming from the emergence of the sketch as a design tool. The first architects to use this method were Francesco di Giorgio Martini . . . and later the architects of the St. Peter's shop, notably Baldassare Peruzzi and Antonio da Sangallo the Younger. (Hewitt 1985, 7)

FIGURE 2-4. Attributed to Benedikt Ried (or Rejt): sketch for the Rider Stair, Old Palace, Hradcany, Prague, Czechoslovakia, about 1503-1505. *Courtesy of Vienna Akademie.*

Users of the new method also included almost all the prominent architects of the sixteenth century, from Bramante to Michelangelo. St. Peter's is not only a landmark for the beginning of the Renaissance but, according to Christof Thoenes's discussion of the early sketches for the building, it is the first building "which can be traced in its development from design drawings . . ." (Thoenes 1982, 82). Thoenes goes on to observe the following:

> We can assume that ever since Daidalos architects have 'always' relied on some kind of drawings. Yet construction of St. Peter's seems to have accorded a new dimension to architectural sketches. [And, in Leonardo's earlier Milan manuscript] we can find the first examples of this new method of sketching in which a (non-existing) building is depicted . . . as if anticipating its actual realization. (82; Thoenes's parentheses)

The manuscript of Leonardo's that Thoenes identifies as the precursor of St. Peter's contains several hypothetical sketches of centralized churches (figure 2-5); these sketches and Bramante's later sketch for St. Peter's (figure 2-6) serve as typical examples of this new approach to drawing in design. Both drawings show the same informal circumstantial scattering of drawings about the page, the same mixture of plan and perspec-

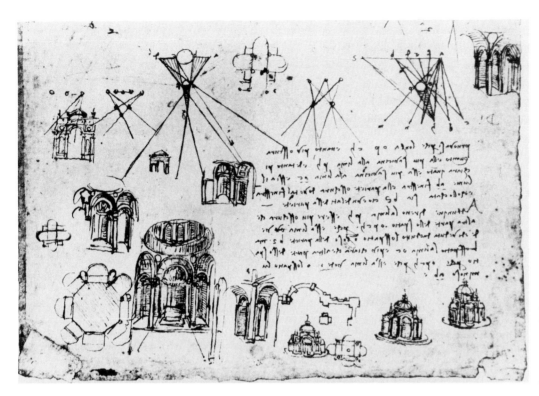

FIGURE 2-5. Leonardo da Vinci: studies for a centrally planned church, about 1508. Ink on parchment. *Courtesy Biblioteca Ambrosiana.*

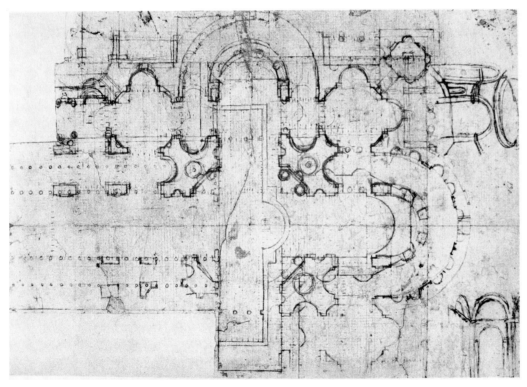

FIGURE 2-6. Donato Bramante: ground plan and sketches for St. Peter's, 1505/06. The page is a composite of several pieces of paper glued together to extend the drawing. Ochre crayon on heavy paper. *Courtesy Galleria degli Uffizi.*

tive views, and the same inquisitive, searching line that invites further exploration. Every aspect of these drawings provides a sharp contrast with the drawings made by medieval architects. Gone are the mechanical drawing instruments. Gone, too, are the geometric rules and

with them the fixed meanings grounded in building craft practices and geometric progressions.

Study drawings made it possible to set out graphic conjectures portraying innovative and not yet existing architectural forms. These graphic conjectures, which might depict a whole building, a part, or a detail, were drawn as freehand fragments; they invited individual interpretation and individual graphic manipulation. Such drawings provided (recalling Gombrich yet again) a beginning schema intended to be a basis for graphic correction, modification, and development; a means to test reality and inquire into the particular.

This was a new design process centered on schematic and developmental operations with study drawings as its principal tool. Like all tools, however, this tool altered the relation of the tool-user to the work. Almost in one stroke, design became separated from the physical act of construction by its emphasis on manipulating graphic symbols, or representations. Regarding the importance of representation in design, Hewitt notes that "from the beginning of the Renaissance mental schemata began to change along with the concept of representation itself" (Hewitt 1985, 7). Fortunately, there is good evidence concerning the mental schemata and concepts of representation of early Renaissance artist-architects—that is, how they might have seen the relation of drawing to an external world.[2] This evidence can be found in the drawings and writings by and about Leonardo.

What did Leonardo have to say about representation? Both his own writing and commentaries on it confirm that Leonardo resolved any doubts about the relation of painting and drawing to external reality by assuming that his graphic representations were direct, transparent expressions of that reality. His description of a painter's relation to nature states his view:

> Painting . . . compels the mind of the painter to transform itself into the mind of nature itself and to translate between nature and art, setting out, with nature, the causes of nature's phenomena regulated by nature's laws—how the likeness of objects adjacent to the eye converges with true images to the pupil of the eye, which of objects equal in size appears larger to that eye; which of equal colors appears more or less dark, or more or less bright, which of objects equally low appears more or less low; which of objects standing at

equal heights will appear more or less high; why, of two objects standing at different distances [from the eye], one will appear less clear than the other. (McMahon 1956, 1;41; McMahon's brackets)

Elsewhere, Leonardo says, ". . . be careful . . . that there is nothing in your work that is not approved by reason or conforms to nature" (Chastel 1961, 197). Chastel also paraphrases Leonardo to say that "observation and memory . . . make the formal truth of things emerge and put the artist at the hub of the relations between the mind and the universe" (192). He notes further that Leonardo,

> . . . after having pushed the relativism which imposes itself on the analysis of phenomena as far as possible, no longer applies it . . . he decides to act as though there were a real color, a real shadow, in short, absolute forms—and painting is exactly the way to represent them (xviii).

If Leonardo believed that media introduced some effect of their own that deviated from exact representation (such as his diagrammatic proof that human stereoscopic vision makes it impossible to reproduce the appearance of a natural model unless the model were seen from a distance or with one eye), he still reproduced the object's appearance as closely as he could, and, like any other painter of his time, ". . . made his flat surface very suggestive of a three-dimensional world and was given credit for doing so" (Baxandall 1962, 33).

On the basis of the evidence from Leonardo it seems possible to conclude that Renaissance architects did regard their drawings as transparent representations of an external, although not yet concrete, reality. This conclusion is of more than passing interest because it establishes a basis for comparison to the way architectural designers use representation today, and thus it becomes a step on the way to understanding the role of study drawings in design.

THE ROLE OF DRAWING IN TODAY'S DESIGN

Five hundred years after Leonardo, artists and architects have gone their almost separate ways. Yet architectural designers in the late twentieth century continue

---

[2]In contrast, I know of no direct evidence that would bear on the assumptions medieval architects might have made about representation.

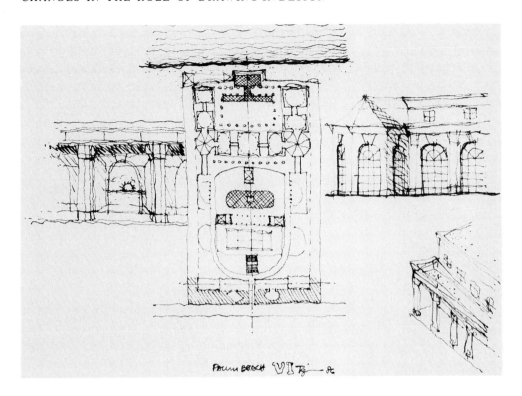

FIGURE 2-7. Stanley Tigerman: sketch for house, Palm Beach, Florida, 1986. Ink on sketchbook page; 8″ × 5″. Number "VI" in a sequence of eight consecutive pages in the sketchbook; see also figure 6-5. *Courtesy Tigerman McCurry Architects.*

FIGURE 2-8. Joseph Esherick: early sketch for California winery, 1989. Pencil on lightweight tracing paper, 36″ × 12″. *Courtesy Joseph Esherick.*

to use study drawings much as architects did in the fifteenth. The sketches of Leonardo and Bramante (figures 2-5 and 2-6) look remarkably modern. Except for the specific details of the project and the drawing surfaces, either of these drawings might have come from Stanley Tigerman's sketchbook (figure 2-7) or Joseph Esherick's folder of study drawings for a California winery (figure 2-8). Tigerman's and Esherick's drawings—and most of the contemporary study drawings in this book—share the same informal approach to composition on the page; the same irregular mix of views, and the same introspective, exploratory line noted above in contrasting Leonardo's and Bramante's drawings with the rigid geometry of the medieval drawings.

Thus the graphic evidence suggests that today's designers use study drawings much as Leonardo and Bramante did. But do today's designers make the same assumptions about representation and transparency? Few contemporary architects have written as much as Leonardo about representation, so understanding their assumptions about the relation between drawing and an external reality needs more inference than Leonardo's explicit statements do.

The five interviews with contemporary architects provide good grounds for such inference. For example, Joseph Esherick's description of his method of making design study drawings in meetings with residential clients (continued from the quotation in chapter 1) suggests that both he and his client assume that they are dealing directly with architectural forms and spaces:

[There are a number of houses that we've done where the client has never seen a complete elevation.] They may have seen parts of it, and understand what it is by putting it together in their minds. They understand the building as it is going to be, not as a model that you look down on and walk around and understand it—bang!—like that. A building . . . [pause] . . . you may never be able to walk around it, may only see it in these little episodic touches. It's because there is the drawing and the explanation at the same time, explanation about purposeful issues, that keeps it from being mysterious.

While Esherick does stress that the verbal explanation is required for the client's understanding, his remarks contain no suggestion that the design process involves any special concern about representation. Helmut Jahn makes a similar statement, with similar implications:

There's a point where in your mind you can't go any further, that you make another drawing. . . . There's nothing extremely intellectual about [drawing], you know, it's just something you've got to test. At the end that's the way buildings get built, with drawings, and the more there is in the drawings the easier it is to build the building. The problems in our profession only come in if the drawings are not good enough, not complete.

Thus, for Jahn, drawing is not problematic in principle: the meaning would always be clear if the drawings were complete. Robert Stern and and Stanley Tigerman raise some doubts about drawing, however. Stern wonders about matters of scale and conventions:

We sit in an office and we draw things for a building that might be twenty times, hundreds of times bigger than the paper. And the relation between the drawing, the sketch or the working drawing, and the big reality is fascinating: How can you imagine a fifty story building when you're working on a three-foot by six-foot desk?

I don't use axonometric because you don't see buildings in axonometric. I was told, by the way, when I was in school that you don't see buildings in elevation; I don't think that's true, that's a modernist prejudice, but plans, sections, elevations, perspectives are still . . . [pause]. I try to use as many different ways of studying the project as possible, including modeling to study the mass outside and the spaces inside; we turn out huge models of important rooms and you can put your head in them. I'm often pleased at the end of the actual construction process that [even though] the building's richer because the materials are better than the foamcore or whatever we were using, the spaces were articulated well in the model.

Stern seems to be in about the same position as Leonardo: to have raised certain questions about the relation of drawing (and models) to external reality, but to have resolved them by joining Leonardo, Esherick, Jahn, and most other architects in assuming that these representations were direct, transparent representations of architectural forms and spaces.

Some architects speak of drawing as more problematic: Tigerman raises the curious issue of drawing, not as representation, but as an end in itself:

So they [i.e., the drawings] don't come to closure, there is an appearance of coming to closure in architecture because you build it. I would say generally you come to closure; something gets built. We [i.e., in my office] try and defer that as long as possible, because I love this stuff and I like to sort of play with it, fondle it, remanipulate it and mold it and knead it and never let [my] hands off it. . . . I don't like finishing buildings. The thing that's interesting to me about what we're doing is the drawing; drawing for me is a way of escaping completion. . . . These kinds of drawings, sketches— drawing is modifying—are my way of avoiding dying. Thinking of the building as the end, I try to avoid the end of the project; when a building is built, it's finally done. I don't like the program, I don't like the building, what I really enjoy is all this, the drawing. These kinds of drawings . . . are what I'm about as an architect, and what I think architecture is about. I don't think architecture is about closure; I think architecture is about modifying.

I go still further: I've always had the feeling that drawing as an activity influences design; so, for example, you'll see sometimes Paul Rudolph will . . . draw in perspective because he actually thinks perspectively, or his buildings at least convey that. So you see Mies van der Rohe's drawings never in perspective; [always in] plan, elevation, section, because he was thinking about planar, about corners, about the meeting of planar elements. You'll see in Richard Meier this almost artificial drawing of an axonometric tilting of the picture plane because that's the way they're working. So I think that the way one draws affects the way the building is designed.

Although it is difficult to make a straightforward inference from Tigerman's "closure" statement regarding his assumptions about representation, his view of drawing clearly is not limited to the instrumental role of transparently representing an external reality. His second statement regarding graphic conventions states that drawing does introduce its own effects into the design process. Thus Tigerman raises the same type of question about the relation of drawing to external reality as did Leonardo and Stern, but he resolves it by making a different assumption: that drawing is not a transparent, neutral representation of architectural forms and spaces; rather, it is a substantial medium that introduces a substantial effect—its own graphic conventions— into the set of design decisions. Still, Tigerman's different assumption about representation and transparency appears not to have affected his approach to making study drawings; these drawings appear to be the same

spirit as those of Esherick, Jahn, and Stern; and, except for the ebullience expressed in both his drawings and his buildings, it appears that he does not attempt to exploit whatever effect drawings have as design issues.

Peter Eisenman made the most specific statement about drawing as a design issue touching on representation and transparency:

PE: What I do is set up a series of ideas or rules or strategies and draw into those, trying to find some form in those ideas. . . . My drawings are rather more haptic or circumstantial and in them I find things that I wouldn't have found if I had said, "This is what I want," to start with.

DH: So the drawing becomes an entity that you read back to yourself. . . .

PE: A true text. It's not the representation of a text, it's the text itself.

Understanding the relation of representation and text suggested in this passage first requires a working definition of the term *text*. Broadly speaking, a text may be defined as an autonomous and integrated system of signification. Applied to architectural study drawings, this use of the term makes three assertions. First, study drawing exists on its own as a system, not dependent on the existence of some building, or even a potential building, for the drawing to represent. Second, drawing has a coherent, systematic set of rules and conventions, something like a written language having its own grammar and syntax. And third, designers have agreed that drawings can signify; that is, they can carry meaning and serve as subjects for interpretation. Thus Eisenman's statement that drawing is "not the representation of a text" asserts that, while buildings may also be texts, drawing does not just act as a secondary text to re-present them. Elsewhere, Eisenman has written about what he calls his "extended" use of the term:

First it must be understood that the extended idea of a text, whether in architecture or not, is the idea of essential multivalence. It does not cancel or deny prior notions of narrative or structure, nor does it necessarily contain them, but exists simultaneously with them. Text never allows a single signified. Everything is shown to mean more than one thing. (Eisenman 1988, 71)

If an architectural drawing is considered as a text, this statement seems to allow it to represent a building, but it does not restrict the drawing to this one function. Furthermore, the statement argues that a drawing cannot signify just one thing; even if it is allowed to signify a building, it must always signify other things, must have more than one meaning.[3] Having more than one meaning keeps drawing from being transparent in the sense defined above, in which the viewer believes that the drawing provides visual access to an external reality without the drawing introducing any effect of its own. If all access to an external reality in architectural graphics must be through some text and no texts are transparent, then the statement suggests that there cannot be any transparent, direct relation to an external reality in design.

Thus Eisenman is a long way from joining Leonardo, Esherick, and Jahn, whose statements imply that their working assumption, along with that of most designers, is that drawing is a transparent representation of an external reality. Eisenman—not alone among contemporary designers[4]—denies such Renaissance-rooted notions of transparency and representation, and he rejects any direct access to external reality. He—again, not alone—also goes beyond Stern's and Tigerman's apparent willingness to leave the working process unchanged; Eisenman deliberately manipulates and exploits the effects of drawing as an explicit design issue, as witnessed by the quotation above about setting up "a series of ideas or rules or strategies" and drawing into them, "to find some form in those ideas."[5]

---

[3]It is true that drawings have multiple meanings after the design task has been completed, but I will argue in chapter 7 that when the designer is acting within the design task, he or she must decide among possible meanings for a drawing, choosing one privileged meaning that will be incorporated in the design as a basis for subsequent decisions.

---

[4]Other contemporary designers who have made drawing an explicit design issue are discussed in chapter 4.

---

[5]Eisenman does not break entirely from the Renaissance approach to drawing, however. In his first drawing for the University of Cincinnati DAAP project (figure 4-10)—intended, he says, to find a graphic strategy—he sets out a schema as a starting point for investigation just as Gombrich described for the postmedieval artist, and just as most other architects do in searching for architectural form. This maneuver raises a new question about what sort of drawing strategy is appropriate to search for a drawing strategy, introducing what seems an infinite regression of drawing to find a strategy for drawing to find a strategy for drawing . . . (etc.).

Making drawing into an explicit design issue concerns both the working process in design and the potential for further changes in the role of drawing. I will put aside considering the working process until chapter 4, and here continue to examine changes in the role of drawing—how drawing is changing today.

POTENTIAL CHANGES IN THE ROLE OF DRAWING IN DESIGN

The discussion above has shown that the transition from medieval to Renaissance design altered the fundamental codes that determined the role of drawing in design, establishing the empirical graphic approach to design still in use today. This approach offered Renaissance designers greater opportunities for graphic manipulation at the cost of increasing the separation of design from construction. Today, new questions concerning representation, transparency, and access to an external reality—questions that challenge the existing fundamental codes—suggest the potential for another change in the relation of drawing to construction.

In the current practice of design, the separation between drawing and construction has two aspects: first, the separation of design from building construction inherited from the Renaissance; and second, a potential major shift—an impending break of design with its own past as architecture catches up with other disciplines in facing questions about the origins of knowledge.

The first aspect, having to do with the inherited separation of design and construction, is a matter of degree. This separation, implicit even in medieval design, increased markedly through the invention of study drawings as a tool for manipulating graphic images. Furthermore, as design has become more professionalized and specialized and as construction has become more technologically complex, the separation has grown even wider. Design has become more completely a graphic discipline, more separate from building construction. Stanley Tigerman addressed this aspect of separation toward the end of the interview on his drawings:

> ST: A drawing has distance from the building, so what is the drawing? The drawing isn't the building. The drawing informs the building, but does it really? It informs other guys who make shop drawings that the building is built from; architects' drawings are not the

instruments from which buildings are made, even their most specific drawing; the shop drawings made by people who are actually going to build the building . . . will say, "Well, this is how I'm going to build it. I've looked at your drawings, Mr. Architect, and this is the way I'm going to do it; I'm not going to do it the way you did it." So architectural drawings have no connection, as opposed to Saussure. Where is the reality? Architects through their own devices and others in society have found themselves more and more removed from building and become more specialized. Architects are more like connoisseurs; we say, "Well, this is better than that," but how this is built is generally not normally the work of drawings made by an architect. A man can go to a shop or a mill and get something drawn and then built; he can look at the drawing himself if he can read drawings and say, "Oh, that's a nice way to do a window, a book, or a this or a that"—he doesn't need an architect in particular. To have an architect is to engage in interpretation, and to interpret takes more time. There is interpretation and there is text; building is a text of texts; drawing is an interpretation of the Modulor, or of the Golden Section, or [it] looks to an earlier period drawn by others, etc. So, drawing is approach avoidance, as the shrinks would call it.

DH: But heretofore, we have had an innocence about what we were doing.

ST: We're no longer so innocent.

DH: I think this loss of innocence has come from linguistics, and I think there is a direct parallel between the drawing . . .

ST: [breaking in] Just as there was in language when the reader was elevated to the same position of authority as the writer. In that period, it's almost like Adam and Eve and God in the Garden when they were brought to parity, there was a problem. The problem was attempted to be resolved in Christianity when hierarchy and [show] displaced forever the need for further interpretation. Architecture is a study of interpretation, like linguistics, like

language, an architectural language like the French language; all these marks that architects make on paper are not so different from the ones that Derrida talks about. They are interpreted because they can be read in different ways, and they are read different ways, but they're not connected to reality, often. People who are involved in reality interpret the architect's drawings and make a final drawing from which it's built, and then the architect is put into a secondary position of one who approves or disapproves the drawing. The architect doesn't make the drawings from which the building is made; he approves or disapproves the drawing made by somebody who knows how to do it.

Tigerman's description overstates the case for separation by neglecting the role Gombrich described: the designer's setting out of a schema as a starting point for corrections and adjustments. In practice, today's architects develop the design to a point where shop drawings can respond to a stated design concept, and where the shop drawings of one trade can be coordinated with those of another.[6]

Nevertheless, the separation of design and construction is still real and still increasing. Shop drawings do provide a bridge of connecting graphic symbols; but rather than narrowing the separation, they widen it even further. Although shop drawing procedures and responsibilities typically are specified in elaborate detail by a set of general conditions for construction contracts, the process often breaks down. Mistakes and misunderstandings are not only frequent but sometimes disastrous. The reaction to such breakdowns in an increasingly litigious business climate is, predictably, to escalate the requirements for shop drawings and to further harden and institutionalize procedures for dealing with them.

While architects often learn a great deal from shop drawings, this learning does not bring the designer closer to the construction of any given project because the learning is displaced. Since the schematic and design

---

[6] *Shop drawings* are the drawings made—usually by building subcontractors for one particular craft, such as precast concrete facing—to show details for shop fabrication, anchorages, connections, etc. These shop drawings are usually submitted to the architect via a general contractor for review as to their conformance with the intent of construction drawings; the architect, in turn, may relay the shop drawing to the appropriate consultant for review.

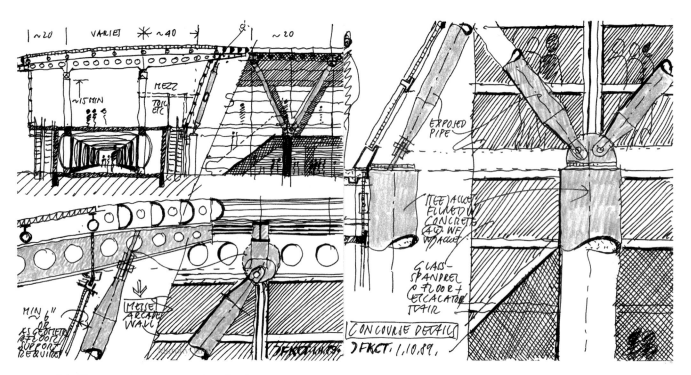

FIGURE 2-9. Helmut Jahn: study drawings for the American Airlines terminal, John F. Kennedy Airport, New York, 1989. Two drawing pages mounted together on one album page. Ink and colored pencil on bond paper; 8½″ × 8½″. *Courtesy Helmut Jahn.*

development study drawings (as well as the architect's construction drawings) have already been completed before the shop drawings appear for that project, the designer's learning from shop drawings must be abstracted and carried forward to some next project. Often this learning also must be transferred from one person to another because the shop drawings may be reviewed by someone other than the project's designer. Such feedback and carry-forward is an essential part of every designer's practical experience, but few designers carry their work into technical detail in the conceptual phases of the work. Thus it is unusual to find study drawings taken as far as Helmut Jahn's highly detailed sketches (figure 2-9).

Just as reliance on shop drawings has grown, architectural construction drawings have increased in comprehensiveness and detail over what they were even a few decades ago. While these kinds of technical drawings also have bridged the separation between study drawings and construction, they have simultaneously widened and formalized it, maintaining the connection between conception and execution only through longer and denser paths of conventionalized symbols and media. The ever-widening separation between drawing and building has allowed designers sometimes to make the

manipulation of graphic figures on the drawing page appear to be an end in itself — as shown, for example, in Michael Graves's elevation studies for the Portland Building (figure 2-10).

At some point this rift between design and construction ceases to be a difference of degree and becomes a difference in kind, leading to the second aspect of separation suggested above: design breaking away from its own past, questioning its own origins of knowledge. The break and questioning do not originate from architecture and are not peculiar to it. Rather the opposite: architecture has come late. Eisenman has noted the following:

In other disciplines, particularly in science and philosophy, there have been extreme changes in the substantive form, the method for producing meaning, since the mid-19th century. . . . While science and philosophy were critically questioning their own foundations, architecture did not. Architecture remained secure in those very foundations derived from philosophy and science that were themselves being rendered untenable by the internal questioning which characterized those disciplines. . . . All of the speculative and artistic disciplines—theology, literature, painting, film and music—have in one way or another come to terms with this dissolution of foundations. . . . What has been called Post-Modernism in architecture . . . has specifically avoided this most important task. (Eisenman 1989, 150)

Although Eisenman is writing here about design, his remarks apply just as directly to graphics for design. Thus the questions raised in this discussion—questions about representation, transparency, and access to an external reality—are part of a larger pattern of change involving many disciplines, a pattern affecting design issues as well as media.

The changes that have occurred in the other disciplines Eisenman mentions have been qualitatively different from earlier changes in that they have addressed the foundations of their own knowledge, giving these changes a self-reflexive cast. Applied to the potential changes in graphics for design, such self-reflection offers a new possibility: changes in media could be consciously designed, rather than incorporated from another discipline as Gombrich and Hewitt described. The directions for future development in design media could involve more deliberate choice than did the changes from the medieval to the Renaissance role of drawing in design.

This choice may not be voluntary, however. It may be forced by a continuing pressure that urges the use of computer graphics in architectural education and practice. I will discuss possible directions for development of computer-aided systems in the appendix; here I will continue the analysis of the only working model available: the existing system of handmade study

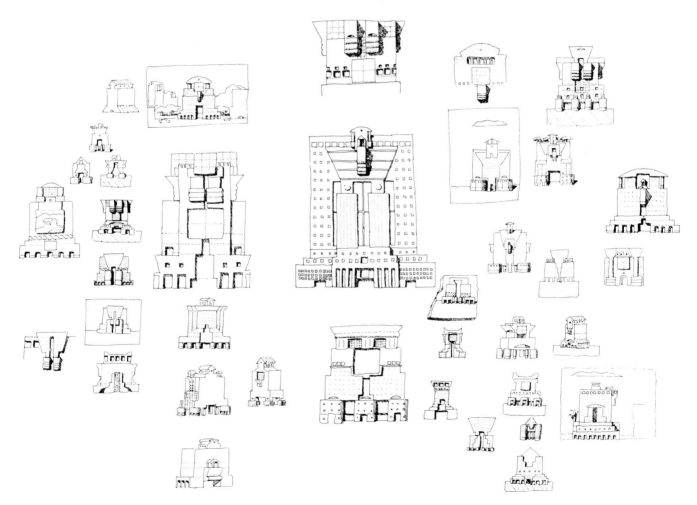

FIGURE 2-10. Michael Graves: facade study drawings for the Portland Building, 1980. *The Portland Building, Portland, Oregon. Preliminary sketches by Michael Graves, Architect. Photo credit: Paschall/Taylor.*

drawings. Only by understanding the operating structure of this system—that is, its properties as a graphic medium for thinking in design—can today's designers make good decisions about its future directions: what to change, what to keep, and, perhaps, how to evaluate a new generation of computer-aided systems. Understanding the properties of study drawings is the task of the following chapters in Part 2.

REFERENCES

Baxandall, Michael. 1972. *Painting and Experience in Fifteenth Century Italy.* New York: Oxford University Press.

Bucher, François. 1968. Design in Gothic architecture, a preliminary assessment. *Journal of the Society of Architectural Historians* 27 (March): 49-71.

Chastel, Andre. 1961. *The Genius of Leonardo da Vinci.* New York: The Orion Press.

Davis, Michael T. 1983. 'Troys portaulx et deux grosses tours': the flamboyant facade project for the cathedral of Clermont. *Gesta* 22 (1): 67-80.

Eisenman, Peter. 1988. Architecture as a second language: the texts of between. *Threshold: Journal of the School of Architecture, University of Illinois at Chicago* 4 (Spring): 71-75.

————. 1989. Blue line text. In *Deconstruction/Omnibus Volume,* ed. A. Papadakis, C. Cooke, A. Benjamin, pp. 150-51. New York: Rizzoli International Publications, Inc.

Foucault, Michel. 1970. *The Order of Things.* New York: Random House.

Gombrich, E.H. 1960. *Art and Illusion.* New York: Pantheon.

Harvey, John. 1950. *The Gothic World.* London: B.T. Batsford, Ltd.

————. 1972. *The Mediaeval Architect.* New York: St. Martin's Press, Inc.

Hewitt, Mark A. 1985. Representational forms and modes of conception. *Journal of Architectural Education* 39 (2): 2-9.

McMahon, A.P. 1956. *Leonardo da Vinci, Treatise on Painting.* Princeton: Princeton University Press.

Thoenes, Christof. 1982. St. Peter's: first sketches. *Daidolos* (September): 81-98.

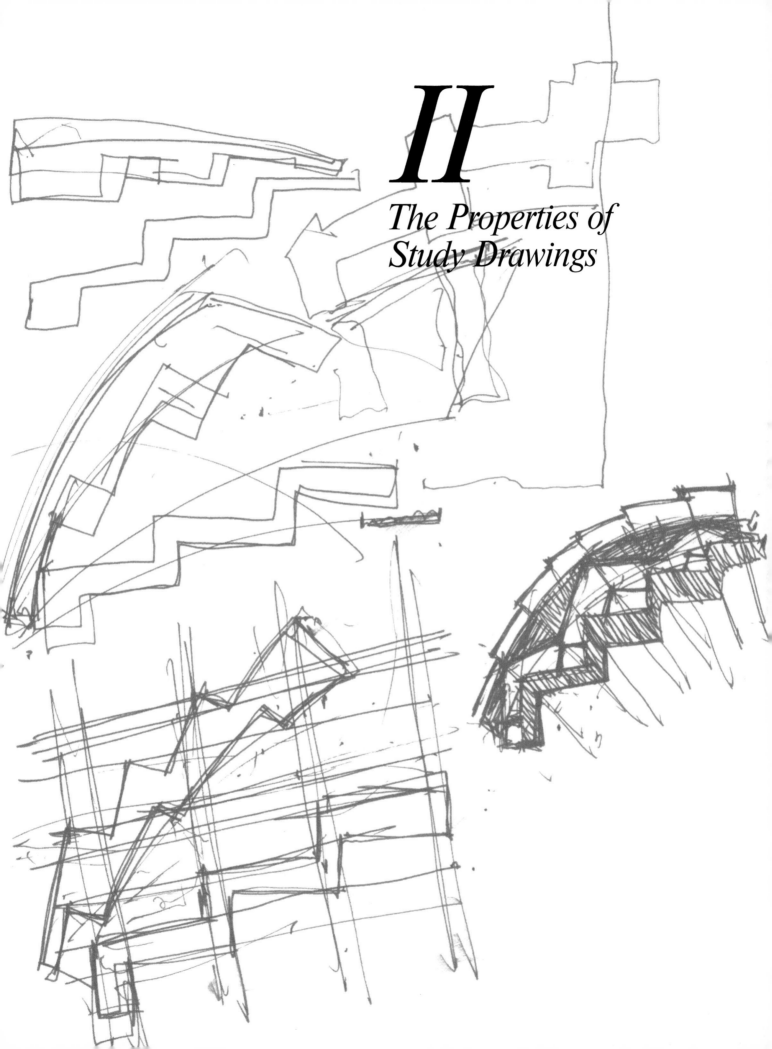

II
The Properties of
Study Drawings

The working process for designing and constructing a building stamps its step-by-step order on everything about architectural practice. But this sequential order is not the same order that Foucault proposes in the epigraph. His version of order comes—pre-existing and marked with violence—from the conditions that make knowledge possible. Thus Foucault's version of pre-existing order is necessarily embodied even in the earliest and most informal study drawings; it obliges designers to assume a world that conforms to their knowledge even at the cost of losing touch with that world.

Acknowledging this order provides a basis for stating the first property of study drawings: *study drawings embody a pre-existing order derived from a background of tacit assumptions and from a loss of information about the design task.*

Le Corbusier's earliest drawings for the chapel of Notre Dame de Ronchamp show how a study drawing can embody the tacit assumptions of a pre-existing order. By his account:

> On the hill I had meticulously drawn the four horizons. There are only four: to the east, the Ballons d'Alsace; to the south, the last spurs leave a vale; to the west, the plain of the Saone; to the north, a small valley and a village. These drawings are missing or lost, it is they which unlocked, architecturally, the echo, the visual echo, in the realm of shape. On the 4th June 1950 . . . Give me charcoal and some paper . . . (Le Corbusier 1957, 89; Le Corbusier's ellipsis)[1]

With his charcoal Le Corbusier drew the first rough version of the chapel plan (figure 3-1). He incorporated his primary concerns in the foreground order of the drawing—that is, his intentions for the organization of architectural forms and spaces on the site. The drawing embodied another kind of order, however: a pre-existing order rooted in a background of assumptions that Le Corbusier, like any other architect, must have tacitly accepted before the drawing began.

3
PRE-EXISTING ORDER

[There is a principle demanding us] not to resolve discourse into a set of preordained significations; not to imagine to oneself that the world turns to us a readable face that we need only decipher simply; the world is not an accessory to our knowledge; there is no pre-discursive providence that disposes things our way. One must conceive discourse as a violence we do to things, or in any case, a practicality we impose on them; and it is in that practicality that the events of a discourse find the principle of their regularity.

MICHEL FOUCAULT

---

[1] Le Corbusier may be taking some license with the date of June 4, 1950, in this passage. The date given for the drawing (No. 4.740) in the *Le Corbusier Archive* is June 6, 1950—a date confirmed by Daniele Pauly's later chronology of the Ronchamp drawings and his essay on Le Corbusier's creative process (Pauly 1980 and 1982).

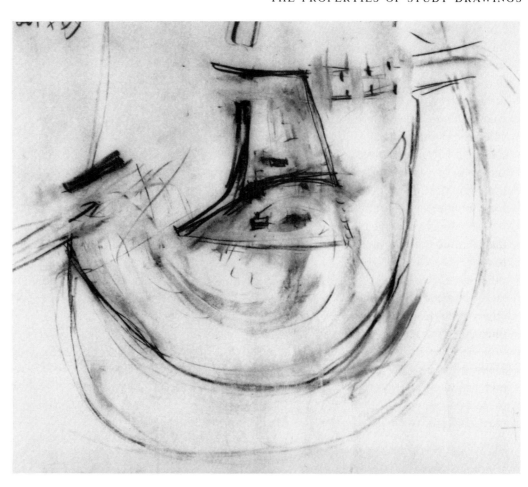

FIGURE 3-1. Le Corbusier: part of a sketch site plan for the chapel at Ronchamp; June 6, 1950 (same as figure 1-7, reprinted here for convenience). © *1922 ARS, N.Y./SPADEM, Paris.*

TACIT ASSUMPTIONS

Le Corbusier himself, the owner's representatives, or some critic or bureaucrat might have identified a few of the tacit assumptions from the drawing's background and written them out as explicit statements:

ARCHITECT AS CREATOR

The architect's role is to be a creator of form, a design specialist who will initiate and lead a design process. In this role the architect is expected to make a uniquely subjective interpretation of the circumstances affecting the design and to express this interpretation in a uniquely subjective design concept. Le Corbusier's recognition of this unspoken assumption is implicit in his "give me paper and charcoal," as well as in his earlier invocation of himself: "Corbu, help them" (Le Corbusier 1957, 88). Such an assumption is embodied not in the particulars of the drawing but in the mere act of making it.

INTEGRATED DESIGN CONCEPT

The various elements of building and site development will be integrated by a unified design concept that expresses a coherent meaning. Le Corbusier (1957, 88) refers to a "solution" and a "theme" for the building; Christian Norberg-Schulz (1975, 408) says of the chapel at Ronchamp: "The synthesis of enclosure and openness not only satisfies the task of making a church, but creates a true 'centre of meaning'. . . ." This assumption of unification is embodied by the drawing's inclusion of the whole project in one sketch, its graphic composition on the page, and the consistent graphic treatment of all its elements; the assumption is further embodied in the subsequent drawings as Le Corbusier's design converges toward a limited and coherent set of forms and materials.

CONVENTIONS

Design proposals will be coded into certain graphic conventions such as plans, sections, elevations, etc. These conventions will be available to incorporate further information from other drawings or from remembered images that have been coded to these conventions, and may be used similarly by other architects to interpret the drawing. Each of these conventions prescribes certain types of lines and a range of possible interpretations for those lines. For early study drawings it is assumed that conformance to conventions is less rigorous than for later drawings; lines are assumed to be both ambiguous and mutable. For example, under the graphic conventions of the plan, Le Corbusier makes three types of lines: those that are intended to represent objects that would be cut by a horizontal plane at chest height, such as the lines that were later developed into walls; those that represent edges of objects or changes in material, such as the lines that were later developed into furniture or site improvements; and those that represent abstract ideas or gestures, such as the arrow at the entrance and other lightly drawn marks. He assumes that all these lines are ambiguous and mutable in that he may reinterpret or ignore any line, or add new lines in this or subsequent drawings.

PROGRAM SUPPORT

The design concept expressed in the drawing will support both an explicit and an implicit program. The architect accepts the explicit program of the liturgy and other stated purposes of the chapel as a legitimate basis for expression in the design concept of this building; e.g., the architectural forms should accommodate the visiting pilgrims, not as individuals but as a congregation, all intended to see a central focus. The owners, the pilgrims, and the architect expect that the design will accommodate elements of the implicit program, even though they are unstated; e.g., the architectural forms will provide for cafe, toilets, telephone, and maintenance services so that it is clear that their functions are not part of the religious program.

SITE RESPONSE

The human purposes of the project will take precedence over geological or biological processes of the site at a small scale but not at a large scale. At Ronchamp, the design may require changing the given form of the hill within certain practical constraints, but not leveling it off to make a mesa; the design may dictate the removal or addition of individual trees, but not removing all vegetation from the hill.

As the examples show, tacit assumptions about design are not inaccessible; it is possible to make explicit statements about them. For theoretical as well as practical reasons, however, the background of tacit assumptions cannot all be made explicit. The background—comprising everything outside the design task—is necessarily inexhaustible, unlimited, unstable, and inevitably shot through with contradictions. To attempt to fix and then formulate such a background into a coherent system of explicit foreground statements would be to defer design forever. It would require an endless and absurd program of stating all possible unstated statements, a preposterous effort to impose a particular order not just on all the unwritten mores and customs of a current design tradition but on the whole experience of the participants in the design project. Thus, for the graphic discourse of any design to go forward there must be a background of unstated, tacit assumptions concerning what practices and commitments can be taken for granted in a particular time and place and what outcomes the participants can expect from the work.

Even though it is impossible to make explicit foreground statements for all the background assumptions, then, the examples from Ronchamp show that it is possible to do so for any given number of them. And the examples show that at least some of the background assumptions embodied by the Ronchamp drawing, when brought forward and stated explicitly, are likely to be acceptable to those of us who are involved in twentieth-century architecture and construction.[2] We are inclined to respect Le Corbusier's role as design expert, and urge him to make the drawing. But, as the examples further show, formulating a statement about any part of the previously tacit background is not neutral; it means identifying a certain issue and taking an ideological position on it—that is, a position that advocates a certain doctrine. The act of taking a position thus creates a

---

[2]In the course of design and construction, owners, users, architects, and builders often find that they do not share the same tacit assumptions. Pauly (1980), for example, suggests that some members of the Ronchamp building committee were not happy with the modern design of the building and most of them thought the building cost too much.

new arguable issue and implies the possibility of considering other, alternative positions.

Alternative positions on previously tacit background issues are more than a theoretical possibility. In the past few years several designers have formulated alternative statements on some of the assumptions stated in the examples given above. These designers have argued for new positions, and have proposed ideological views that vary from those commonly accepted in the field. For example, Christopher Alexander has questioned the role of the architect as creator and proposed a more modest role (Alexander, Ishekawa, and Silverstein 1977). Peter Eisenman has contested the assumption of the single, strong, integrated design concept and challenged certain drawing conventions (Eisenman 1989). Bernard Tschumi has rejected program and physical setting as appropriate or exclusive bases for design, and he has explored design proposals that disrupt rather than serve the functional program (Tschumi 1989). Such alternative positions assign other, different meanings to the ensuing study drawings, whether the alternative positions are explicitly formulated as special exceptions to our own conventional design assumptions—like those of Alexander, Eisenman, and Tschumi—or, perhaps, tacitly accepted as background conditions for some alien practice.

The consequences of these alternative positions would necessarily be embodied graphically in an alternative discourse of design. Under Alexander's unorthodox position about the interaction between client and architect, for example, Le Corbusier might not have made the first drawing for Ronchamp; instead, he might have physically staked out functional areas on the site, or helped a group of the owners' representatives to do so. Or, perhaps, under Eisenman's approach to site organization, the owners' representatives would have expected Le Corbusier to draw an extension of the nearby railway line to disrupt the "natural" site. If Le Corbusier had subscribed to Tschumi's notion of disruption, he could have drawn the pilgrims' gathering place as dispersed and uncontained, or overlaid it with a stand of trees that deliberately interfered with sightlines to the outside altar.

That these propositions seem extreme is exactly to the point: any design discourse requires an unnoticed "natural" and "normal" order, a background of tacit assumptions against which most exceptions seem extravagant and even violent. Foucault reminds us, however, that our own version of a natural order is no innocent

account of an objective reality; our version is itself just as extravagant and violent as any exceptions to it, as dogmatic as any alien order. It is an artifact, an imposition of our own notions of practicality on the world: "there is no prediscursive providence that disposes things our way . . . ," or waits faithfully for our knowledge to reflect them.

These comments about the background order apply not just to Ronchamp but to any design project. Frank Gehry's first sketch for his house (figure 3-2) and Peter Eisenman's conceptual studies for the Columbus Convention Center (figure 1-16) appear just as unconstrained and free to address their author's immediate concerns as Le Corbusier's sketch. Whatever differences these two may have from each other or from Le Corbusier about some design issues, both Gehry's and Eisenman's drawings embody some set of tacit assumptions that allows the work to proceed. Both drawings, for example, are evidence for their authors' assumptions that the architect is a subjective, creative presence, that lines may be taken to represent objects, or that a competent construction technology will be available to execute their design.

The background order of study drawings is not limited to assumptions about such general or comprehensive concerns; it also includes assumptions about specific situations. Gehry, in choosing to add a group of spaces to one side of this house, for example, has accepted assumptions about nearby houses, streets, building codes, etc. Similarly, in making the drawings for the Convention Center project, Eisenman has accepted a given site and a program for the competition, loading each drawing with additional assumptions about ownership, access, orientation, neighborhood character, budget, etc., that apply to this project. Such a tacit assumption might be formulated by saying, "Vehicular access for this site will rely on perimeter surface streets." This example shows that unless one wishes to take exception to some tacit assumption, stating it is unnecessary—it merely says what would seem obvious to residents of midwestern American cities in the late twentieth century: vehicles use streets. Yet every design project does involve some exceptions that must be brought forward from the amorphous background. At Ronchamp, Le Corbusier meticulously draws the four horizons, a drawing that he says unlocked the architectural shape of the project. For the Columbus Convention Center, Eisenman makes a distinction between service and passenger vehicles and builds that distinction into his conceptual sketch.

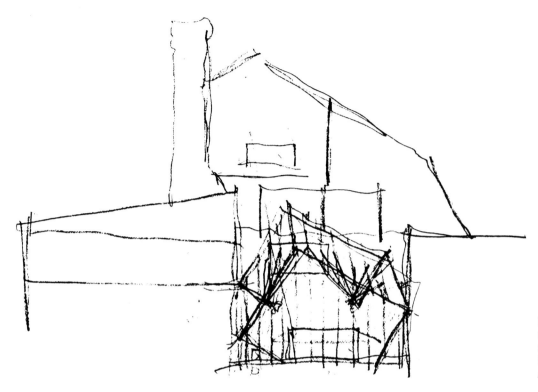

FIGURE 3-2. Frank Gehry: early sketch for Gehry house addition, Santa Monica, California, 1978. *Courtesy Frank O. Gehry.*

For any given project, then, some exceptions must be brought forward, either verbally or graphically, as explicit foreground statements that specify the ways in which some aspect of the project might differ from the tacit background. These new exceptions then join the body of already accepted, or sanctioned, foreground statements that make up the design task—the convenience of users in getting from one space to another, or the location of stairways and exits, for example. Such sanctioned statements have previously been identified and formulated from a tacit background, their acceptance as foreground issues has been negotiated among designers (or, in the case of building code requirements, imposed by law), and they have been confirmed by education and practice as "natural" and "appropriate"[3];

[3]In contrast, an example of an architect's design statement not sanctioned by practice would be a drawing for a building that would deliberately mislead users as to how to enter it. An unsanctioned programmatic statement would be an owner's request to an architect to build a copy of Ronchamp for, say, a savings and loan office. This is not to suggest that these statements could not be made, but they would, in the last half of the twentieth century, be outside the design tradition that expects architects to "tell the truth" to a building's users and limits savings and loan copies of historic buildings to secular prototypes such as Mount Vernon or Independence Hall.

they constitute the continually changing design tradition of any time and place.

The design tradition in current Western architectural practice provides several ways for new exceptions to the tacit background to be brought forward and included as foreground statements for a particular project. A users' group or owners' representative might make such statements (most often verbally) to the architect in a list of program requirements, ranging from the specific—say, the need to isolate a certain laboratory area from traffic vibration—to the very general—say, vague expressions concerning light or openness. And, throughout the design work, the architect brings forward other new exceptions, both verbal and graphic, as foreground statements to join the previously accepted ones. The manipulation of such statements on the drawing page, along with their interpretation, may be said to constitute the events of the design discourse.

Graphic statements play the principal role in this discourse. To be included, verbal statements by the architect or anyone else must eventually be transformed into graphic statements. Verbal statements may be transformed into graphic ones either directly by means of design synthesis drawings as shown in the drawings above by Le Corbusier, Gehry, and Eisenman, or indirectly by other more analytic drawings—the abstract diagrams designers use to study or illustrate the relationships of one or two aspects of the design task. Such verbal-to-graphic transformations in analytic drawings are evident in space adjacency diagrams (figure 3-3) and site analysis diagrams (figure 3-4).[4]

In transformation from a verbal to a graphic notation, an analytic statement may be a composite of graphic marks and written notes, as in the site analysis diagram. But, because the graphic context of the diagram governs the meaning and purpose of the notes, they become essentially graphic rather than essentially verbal statements. A note in a composite diagram such as the "shortcut" note on the site analysis diagram would change or lose its meaning if placed elsewhere on the diagram, and though part of this note is written as a complete sentence, its purpose is not just to convey a certain meaning but to incorporate that meaning at a specific location on the developing drawings.

Making a graphic statement—either composite or purely graphic—has many of the discursive strengths and weaknesses of a verbal statement. For analytic diagrams, the decision to bring any issue, such as the shortcut, forward out of the background order and formulate an explicit graphic statement about it advocates a particular position on a certain ideological issue: the shortcut drawing and note assert that part of the design task for this project is to consider the circumstances of neighborhood use in minute detail, an issue on which an architect or an owner might plausibly take a different position.

Aside from whether one agrees with their ideological content, graphic statements like the shortcut drawing have a seductive appeal because they are largely pictorial, and the designer's architectural training invites him or her to accept them as objective and transparent representations of an external reality. Yet representation is always problematic. In the site analysis diagram, for example, the line representing the shortcut and its adjacent note are subjective interpretations, artifacts of whatever assumptions and experience the observer has brought to that part of the design task. A less acute

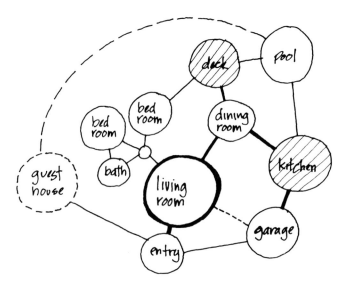

FIGURE 3-3. Paul Laseau: example of space adjacency diagram. *Courtesy Paul Laseau.*

observer might not notice the shortcut at all; a more subtle or sophisticated observer might understand the shortcut as the key to unlock a complex network of paths that holds the neighborhood together.

Even more subjective and interpretive than analytic diagrams are the design synthesis drawings: the Ronchamp sketch not only brings forward more design issues than the narrowly focused analytic diagram, but it also brings them forward more ambiguously to serve as open-ended statements for a next round of interpretations in the design sequence. For both the analytic diagram and the design synthesis drawing, the inescapable choice to draw one thing rather than another means that graphic statements are no less an imposition of practical order; no less violent, strange, or ideological than are the verbal statements Foucault considered. Neither the analytic diagram nor the design synthesis drawing is a more innocent account of objective reality than is a purely verbal description; they all embody ideological positions on issues selected as exceptions to a supposedly natural background of tacit assumptions.

Thus the foreground drawings reflect the designer's interactions with the background of tacit assumptions in two senses: first, all foreground statements—both new and previously sanctioned statements—originate as exceptions to the tacit background; and second, foreground drawings are interpreted against the tacit background. In both senses, interaction with the background becomes part of the drawing's meaning. The

---

[4]Note that analysis diagrams also may go through rough and finished stages; see figure Int-1 for a "rough sketch" of a space adjacency diagram. These rough sketches resemble rough sketches in design synthesis drawings, except that in the rough diagram the designer is searching for the appropriate form of the diagram rather than the appropriate form of a building.

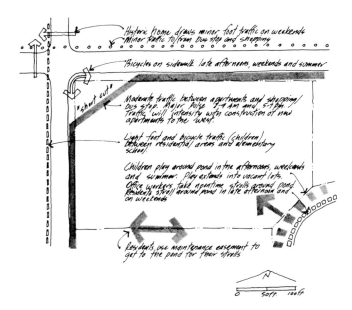

FIGURE 3-4. Edward T. White: example of site analysis drawing. *Courtesy Edward T. White.*

graphic discourse of design is a sequence of the designer's making and then interpreting study drawings, with the meaning of each act of drawing and each interpretation colored by its interaction with the background. Furthermore, these interactions also change the tacit background as parts of it become explicit foreground statements.

This tension between foreground statements and their elusive background is not confined to design; critics Hubert Dreyfus and Paul Rabinow describe a similar situation in contemporary philosophy: "Discourse about man faces the following dilemma: the background of taken-for-granted commitments and practices, precisely because it is unthought, makes thought and action possible, but it also puts their source and meaning out of our control" (Dreyfus and Rabinow 1982, 37). Dreyfus and Rabinow's remark neglects interactions with the background, but their main point does apply to design: the tacit background assumptions of study drawings make foreground graphic thought and action possible but it also puts their source and meaning out of the designer's full control. Although designers can select and engage specific issues derived from the background, they can never comprehend or control it as a whole, for it recedes like a horizon from every attempt to approach it. Study drawings' explicit foreground is always isolated from their tacit background, then, even as the drawings embody a pre-existing order derived from interactions with that background.

How can interactions with the background provide order when the background is itself essentially unordered?[5] The answer lies not in the order of the background but in the order of the interactions. Since these interactions can exist only as formulations of a graphic medium, it is the medium—that is, study drawings—that finally gives order to the interactions. Here the term *embody* takes on a surprising new meaning: as study drawings embody the order of the tacit background, the order that is embodied comes not from the background but from the study drawings.

This active role of the graphic medium is only one of the surprises hidden in the pre-existing order of study drawings. A second surprise is that these interactions with the background and the ensuing manipulation of statements in the foreground actually lose information about the design task.

INFORMATION LOSS

It seems paradoxical to associate a deliberately creative act, which making study drawings undoubtedly is, with a loss of information. Indeed, chapters 4 and 5 will show that thought and action by means of study drawings are the principal means of generating information in design. Nevertheless, the loss of information about the design task is a part of the pre-existing order of study drawings in action, an inevitable consequence of every move the designer makes. Below I will discuss three kinds of information loss: two concerning interactions with the tacit background and one concerning manipulations in the always-evolving foreground of the design task.

The first kind of information loss has to do with the quantitative limitations of action in design. In theory it is possible to make any number of explicit foreground

[5]It may be objected that other parts of the designer's surroundings have their own foreground order, rather than being essentially unordered. This may be true, but whatever foreground order they may have is not organized as architectural design information (if it were, it would be architectural design). Thus, until some part of that order is engaged through the interactions described in this discussion, the foreground order of other disciplines must be considered as part of the tacit background for design. A corollary of this point is that design is a part of the tacit background for every other discipline—suggesting a complex metaphor of multivalent interacting foregrounds, rather than the simpler metaphor of a univalent foreground ordered against an amorphous background that I have used in this discussion.

statements through interaction with the infinite tacit background, but in practice the number of such statements is limited. Not all statements can be made, not all information developed; some must be left behind. The need to leave some background assumptions unidentified, unformulated, and thus unexamined produces one straightforward type of information loss: it means losing information by default—the information about previously tacit assumptions (and their alternatives) that might have been developed, or the information that would have been produced by incorporating all possibilities into the work. At Ronchamp, for example, it would have taken Le Corbusier forever to draw all the details of all the horizons visible from the site, and it would have been impossible to pursue both his own design approach toward expressive form and a mutually exclusive alternative approach of restoring the previous building.

Whether undeveloped assumptions and unexplored possibilities—the unthought background that Dreyfus and Rabinow described—can be said to have existence enough to be considered "lost" information is a moot point. It is the unthought background that makes thought and action possible, so the need to decide, on the basis of information known to be incomplete, which design concept to pursue and build does impose a pre-existing order on a designer's study drawings. In the working process, this order limits the possible meanings that can be attributed to the marks on the drawing page: it affects the next marks the designer will make. Thus the problem of incomplete information and limited possibilities requires that designers learn—always within a particular design tradition at a particular time—how to sort through different conceptual approaches and when to stop developing information as a basis for design decisions.

Closely related to these quantitative losses are the second kind of information losses. These are qualitative losses that come from inescapable choices about relevance—about what ought to be ignored and what brought to the foreground of the design task.

Le Corbusier's charcoal drawing for Ronchamp illustrates his choices about what to ignore and what to bring forward. As he made the drawing, Le Corbusier could have identified and formulated an endless amount of information about the project, ranging from the bearing capacity of the previous chapel's old stone to the demographics of the local village, from the character of the access road to the average snowfall in the region, from the contours of the hill to the patterns of

calcination and scorching on the old building's ruined walls. And, as for any project at any time, there might have been other unknown but possibly significant factors such as the effects of future earth movement, religious factions, acid rain, and global warming.[6] Le Corbusier's drawing clearly shows his principal concerns, however: the road, the slope, the exterior spaces. In his subsequent design drawings he deals with other matters: the bearing capacity of the old stones, the shapes of openings, the thicknesses of walls. Still other matters he continued to ignore: the number of teenagers in the village, global warming, and, probably, patterns on the old walls. Le Corbusier's situation was not unique: the need to make such choices about what to develop from an unlimited tacit background faces all architects.

Besides making choices about data related to the surroundings, architects must make choices about program data. Most have had to work with and learn to discount overdefined programs that say too much, for example, by listing area requirements to fractions of a square foot. Other programs specify commonplace activities in excess detail or bring up issues that cannot affect architectural decisions. Choosing relevant information from the tacit background means losing potential information by leaving it behind. Before writing off this loss as inconsequential just because it involves only irrelevant information, it is necessary to ask how architects make choices about what is relevant for their work in design.

Choices about relevance might be thought of as introducing a sort of mediating grid into the working process. This grid imposes a particular structure on everything the designer considers: program, physical surrounding, form, meaning, even what will be considered as offering the potential for coding into meaning. Four centuries before Le Corbusier's drawing, for example, when signs from nature were sought out and studied as manifestations of God's will,[7] it is possible

---

[6]Although Le Corbusier surely could not have known about global warming, he might have insisted that new information about seismic activity at the site was necessary for him to proceed with the work. An architect in 1993 might very well decide that information about the potential for acid rain at Ronchamp—no doubt unknown to Le Corbusier—would be needed as foreground data.

[7]Foucault (1970, 59) says, "[In the sixteenth century] signs were thought to have been placed upon things so that men might be able to uncover their secrets . . . the task [of knowledge] was to uncover a language which God had previously distributed across the face of the earth. . . ."

that patterns of scorching found on the old stones would have given a Renaissance Le Corbusier vital information needed to design the new building. Four centuries from now, perhaps, architects will consider access roads and natural signs from God less (or more) relevant than they do now. At any given time, the grid gives architects a fair idea of what is relevant for a design task. Some selection from unlimited information is essential for any design process to go forward, and only some kind of imposed grid makes selection possible.

Although the grid seems both transparent and neutral, it is neither. It imposes serious effects not limited to information loss. The grid intrudes itself; it has a presence, a substance, and a grain that permit it to reveal only certain things, to obscure others, and to add its own bias to the world as it allows selection and ordering. (Le Corbusier asks for a contractor's opinion about the road, but not for a seer's interpretation of patterns on the old stones.) Furthermore, the grid forces intention: selection must have a purpose. Data intended for use in design will differ from data for administration, and data for designing a chapel will be inappropriate for designing a school. Both of these effects of the grid lose information by selection, as if through a complex system of sieves. These are qualitative choices, different from the simpler quantitative losses described above.

Beyond the grid is a still more complex type of information loss, however, a most un-seivelike action that causes the third and most complex kind of information loss. This action is related to the graphic manipulations of the drawing's explicit foreground order. To see how such manipulations can incur a loss of information requires turning briefly from graphics to science.

In recent decades, issues related to the structure of systems have commanded attention in many disciplines. In the biological sciences, for example, neurobiologist Gunther Stent has summarized a body of experimental findings on the structure-building processes of the human nervous system (Stent 1978). Stent describes abstraction, or the selective destruction of information, as one of the system's basic principles of operation:

The processing of data by the [intercranial part of the nervous system] consists in the main in making an abstraction of the vast amount of data continuously gathered by the sensory part. This abstraction is the result of a selective destruction of portions of the input data in order to transform these data into manipulable categories that are

meaningful to the animal. It should be noted that the [operation of the nervous system] depends not only on the here-and-now sensory inputs, but also on the history of past inputs. Stated more plainly, neurons can learn from experience. (158-59)

Stent goes on to note the mechanics of the nervous system's selective destruction of information through abstraction, using the visual system as an illustration. He describes how the amount of light on particular cells of the retina are transformed into a more abstract report of light-dark contrast (162-65). Elsewhere, he points out that the effect of making structures goes beyond the operation of that system:

For the mind, reality is a set of structural transformations of primary data taken from the world. This transformation process is hierarchical in that "stronger" structures are formed from "weaker" structures through the selective destruction of information. Any set of primary data becomes meaningful only after a series of such operations has so transformed it that it has become congruent with a stronger pre-existing structure in the mind. (111)

Whether structural transformations are the only reality for the mind is beyond the scope of this discussion. Stent makes a good case, however, for believing that the mind does not have direct access to an objective reality through the senses, and that information must be lost through abstraction at any level of any mental activity, from the simplest act of perception to the creation of the broadest conceptual structures.

Stent's description provides the mechanics to complement the theoretical and critical analysis of information loss. Applied to the working processes of design, the neurobiological account helps to explain both the loss of information and the creation of meaning in study drawings. This view of abstraction implies that the circumstances the designer intends to address can be apprehended only indirectly, through the successive structure-building abstractions of the visual system. Each successive abstraction transforms new structures into congruence with structures based on previous experience; incongruent information is lost through selective destruction. Meaning requires making structures; but making structures always involves abstraction and so always loses information. Thus, the loss of information about the circumstances surrounding the design

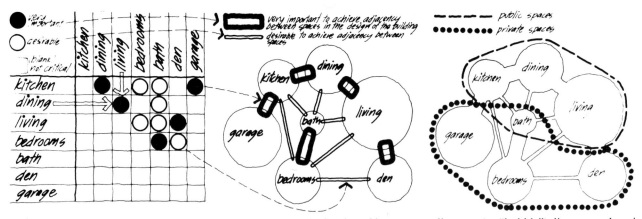

FIGURE 3-5. Edward T. White: example of space adjacency matrix developed into space adjacency (or "bubble") diagram and zoning diagram. *Courtesy Edward T. White.*

task could be termed the cost of acquiring meaning in design study drawings.

Combining concepts from these critical and scientific disciplines now makes it possible to analyze specific examples of study drawings. Before considering the complexities of design synthesis drawings, the analysis had best take up the simpler case of analytic drawings.

One type of analytic study drawing is actually a trio of diagrams: the architectural adjacency matrix, the "bubble" diagram, and the zoning diagram (the bubble diagram is similar to the adjacency diagram discussed above). Such diagrams have been developed into refined design tools by Edward T. White (1986), and appear here only in their simplest form (figure 3-5). Adjacencies required between individual rooms (or spaces) are shown in the matrix and then transformed into the bubble diagram. The bubbles are abstract representations of entities—here, the rooms of a house—usually scaled in rough proportion to area and often modified by hatching or line weight to suggest some quality such as acoustic isolation; the lines between the bubbles represent relationships between the entities—in these diagrams, the need for adjacency—with the degree of need for adjacency represented by thickness of the lines. In the zoning diagram, bubbles are grouped according to some criteria such as "public" and "private."

The adjacency diagram loses information at every turn (again, note that chapters 4 and 5 will consider how such graphic conceptual structures also generate information). The loss of information is most evident in the diagram's use of abstract terms. Both kinds of terms included in the diagram—entities such as rooms and relationships such as adjacency—are abstractions, having already incurred several levels of selective destruction of information. To take an example, a kitchen

contains hundreds of activities that are unspecified by the term (which in practice the diagram tacitly assumes to mean "space for storing, preparing, and sometimes serving food"). The details of idiosyncratic and specialized uses of a specific kitchen by specific persons and groups—such as for study, home office work, conversation, or recreation—are lost through the same principles of summation and averaging that transform data in the visual system. Similarly, the term *adjacency* transforms data about many details of time, quality, purpose, or sequence into an abstract conventional relationship between two spaces.

The adjacency diagram also loses information through manipulation of its terms: it selects only one structure of relationships and loses the potential information in all the structures not portrayed. For example, many of the conventional relationships shown in the diagram, as well as the conventional zoning from public to private, could change markedly during a child's illness or a family quarrel. Although another diagram could accept the new relationships, or any given number of new relationships that were not mutually exclusive, no diagram can represent adjacencies for all possible relationships. Adding explanatory notes can make up for some losses, but notes are themselves new abstractions selected from an endless amount of information about the project.

It might seem that the problem of lost information from using such elements as spaces could be eliminated by moving the analysis to a more detailed level—say, to *activity centers* within the spaces, or, at a still more detailed level, to *activities* within the activity centers. Going into detail does not solve the problem, however, as the following analysis will show: in another part of his work on adjacency analysis, White (1986) has provided a means for moving the analysis from one level to another—a hierarchical diagram of levels of detail (or abstraction) for a hypothetical industrial project (figure 3-6). The diagram shows that the hierarchy could be extended to upper levels that White calls *functional components* and *departments,* or to lower levels such as *activities.*[8] Conceivably, the levels could go still lower (not shown in White's diagram), perhaps to *operations, tools, parts, materials, molecules,* etc. A bubble diagram similar to that of figure 3-5 could be made for an entity at any level—say, the *activity center* level, composed of the entities at the next lower level: *sitting, reading,* etc. The information loss has not disappeared, however. While activities such as sitting and reading are less abstract than entities such as spaces, they are still high-level abstractions with their own losses of information.

Furthermore, moving down the hierarchy causes another type of information loss through reduction. Going from the upper level to start the analysis at the *activity* level means losing the way back, since no amount of interaction at the lower level can make a higher entity without an external and intentional act of combination, selecting certain elements and formulating them as new entities—thus introducing another abstraction. Moving even further down the hierarchy involves the same analysis: *sitting* as an entity might break down to more detailed entities like *posture, time, frequency,* etc.: all still abstractions from experience. Each move lower in search of a solid ground under the abstraction fails to eliminate the problem of information loss because abstraction persists as a condition of knowledge. Each move lower through the hierarchy incurs the effect of

reduction as higher-level structures disappear. The structure of the analytic diagram, then, allows the organization of information that we call knowledge, but only at the cost of information lost through abstraction. Abstraction renders knowledge possible.

The mechanics of information loss apply to design synthesis drawings as well as to analytic diagrams. I will return to Le Corbusier's Ronchamp drawing yet again, now to look for evidence of abstraction and its consequences.

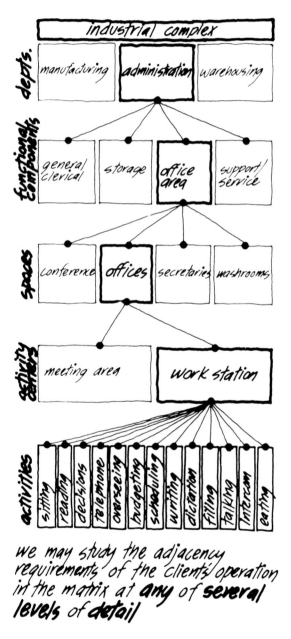

FIGURE 3-6. Edward T. White: diagram illustrating equivalent levels of detail. *Courtesy Edward T. White.*

---

[8]Several problems are immediately apparent as the levels of the diagram in figure 3-6 are extended into more detail. First, at lower levels of the diagram, identifying equivalent entities becomes impossible: is *reading* an equivalent entity to *budgeting? sitting* to *intercom?* Second, extension of the diagram either up or down becomes increasingly arbitrary as to the class of entities. What class lies below *activities* depends on one's intention: the entities might be *positions* if one were designing furniture, or *operations* if one were managing personnel. Third, the quantities quickly become unmanageable. For example, it is theoretically possible to consider all the elements in the whole hierarchy—from, say, the *activities* level up to the *departments* level in a series of nested diagrams. Then the total number of elements at the activities level required for the diagram would be $3 \times 4 \times 5 \times 2 \times 13 = 1560$. This is far too many elements to comprehend because the number of interrelations among 1560 elements in a relationship matrix is 1,216,020. If a designer were to evaluate and record one relationship intersection every 30 seconds, it would take more than two years of steady and excruciatingly boring work to complete the matrix.

For the programmatically simple chapel at Ronchamp, Le Corbusier had no need to make a space adjacency matrix or diagram; he had no need even to name the spaces as he drew them, so the drawing does not contain the same kinds of specific entities and relationships as the analytic drawings. Nevertheless, the Ronchamp drawing, too, is abstract in the sense of the earlier discussion about tacit assumptions: that choosing to draw one thing rather than another involves the selection and ordering that always creates abstract structures. The drawing is abstract also in the sense that it is composed of a particular organization of lines, made with intention and according to certain conventions, and embodying such apparent abstractions as the entrance space, the congregation space for pilgrims to witness certain rites, a very conventional arrow at the south gate, and a particular orientation for the building. Le Corbusier, in his description of the missing first drawings of the "four horizons," gave special significance to the abstract cardinal points of the compass ("There are only four . . . "). With respect to its loss of information about the circumstances that initially prompted the drawing, then, the design synthesis drawing is similar to the abstract structure of the analytic drawing.

The abstract structure of the design synthesis drawing differs from that of the analytic drawing in two respects, however. First, in comparison with the analytic drawing, with its explicit, discrete entities and relationships arranged in a set format, the elements of the design synthesis drawing are neither explicit, nor discrete, nor entities, because all areas of the page are both entities and relationships whose format is indeterminate. Abstraction, as selection and ordering, depends on explication, and the design synthesis drawing stops short of full explication. Elements of the Ronchamp drawing seem explicit; they can be pointed to and named—"entrance space," "congregation space," etc.—as in the discussion above; but the names are far more explicit and therefore more abstract than their referents in the drawing. To the extent that the drawing is inexplicit and ambiguous, it is open to multiple interpretation, and it is exactly these multiple interpretations that allow further development of the design. When design synthesis drawings are no longer ambiguous, the design development stops. The discussion on tacit assumptions, above, noted that design synthesis drawings bring design issues forward more ambiguously than analytic drawings, to serve as open-ended statements for the next cycle of interpretations in the design sequence.

Abstraction in design synthesis drawing differs from that of analytic drawing in a second respect, which also has to do with cycles of interpretation: interpretation and drawing take real time.[9] Even such quick sketches as the Ronchamp drawing start with a particular mark on the page; this mark immediately becomes a new element in the conceptual scope of the design task as well as on the drawing page, so that each next line is made in response to all its predecessors. This response is not a simple reaction, but an ongoing complex cycle of perception, interpretation, invention, feedback, and graphic composition on the page. For the study drawing, each mark must offer the ambiguity that allows the cycles to continue rather than stop. I will take up this complex cycle with its essential graphic ambiguity in detail in the next chapters, but will remark here that within each cycle there is a continuing abstraction as the eye, mind, and hand attempt to acquire and enhance meaning at the cost of lost information.

Information loss in study drawings is inevitable, then. Both the design synthesis drawing and the analytic diagram always lose information about the circumstances surrounding the design task. This loss occurs first at a simple default level by dropping out foregone assumptions, next at a more complex level by a cultural grid's selection of data for relevance, and finally at a still more complex level through the formation of abstract structures whose meaning can only be understood by becoming congruent with previous experience. Moreover, the information loss from making structures is not a one-time cost; it must be paid each time structures are combined or revised to create new and more comprehensive organizations, at each step in the creation of the compound hierarchical structures we call study drawings. Through this abstraction and information loss even the first study drawings are separated from the always unreachable source of perceptions.

These new observations concerning meaning and information loss through abstraction provide a useful supplement to the earlier discussion about tacit assumptions. Now it is possible to say that the foreground statements only acquire their initial meaning by abstraction from the background of tacit assumptions. Thus the foreground statements of the design embody the background because at least part of the data about

---

[9]Most critiques of drawings, whether of conceptual sketches or presentation drawings, consider the finished drawing only, and treat it as an object: single, whole, and complete.

the design task has been abstracted from that background. It is also possible to add confirmation that our own version of a natural order is not an innocent account of some presumed objective reality. In accord with Foucault's observation, our version is an artifact, an imposition of our own practical distinctions and order on the world, and study drawings provide the sole means for introducing these practical distinctions and order into the discourse of design. To get on with the work of design, we must impose distinctions and order; we must lose information about, and so become separated from, the circumstances that we seek to engage with the design. Although we cannot avoid the discussion's harsh theme—the loss of information, the separation of design from its roots, the imposition of order—it is also possible to confirm that design is more full of choices, richer, and more engaging then we could have thought.

REFERENCES

Alexander, Christopher, Sara Ishikawa, and Murray Silverstein. 1977. *A Pattern Language: Towns, Buildings, Construction.* New York: Oxford University Press.

Dreyfus, Hubert, and Paul Rabinow. 1983. *Michel Foucault, Beyond Structuralism and Hermeneutics.* Chicago: University of Chicago Press.

Eisenman, Peter. 1989. En terror firma: in trails of grotextes. *Deconstruction/Omnibus Volume,* ed. A. Papadakis, C. Cooke, A. Benjamin, pp. 152-53. New York: Rizzoli International Publications, Inc.

Foucault, Michel. 1970. *The Order of Things.* New York: Random House.

Le Corbusier. 1957. *The Chapel at Ronchamp.* New York: Frederick A. Praeger.

Norberg-Schulz, Christian. 1975. *Meaning in Western Architecture.* New York: Praeger Publishers.

Pauly, Daniele. 1980. *Ronchamp, Lecture d'une Architecture.* Paris: A.P.P.U.; Ophrys.

———. 1982. The Chapel of Ronchamp as an example of Le Corbusier's creative process. *The Le Corbusier Archive.* Vol. 20, *Ronchamp, Maisons Jaoul, and Other Buildings and Projects,* pp. ix-xix. New York: Garland Publishers; Paris: Fondation Le Corbusier.

Stent, Gunther. 1978. *Paradoxes of Progress.* San Francisco: W. H. Freeman and Company.

Tschumi, Bernard. 1989. Parc de la Villette, Paris. *Deconstruction/Omnibus Volume,* ed. A. Papadakis, C. Cooke, A. Benjamin, pp. 175-81. New York: Rizzoli International Publications, Inc.

White, Edward T. 1986. *Space Adjacency Analysis.* Tucson, Ariz.: Architectural Media Ltd.

At a few years' remove, even the architect found it hard to trace the sources of his work. The chapel at Ronchamp is the most fully documented of Le Corbusier's projects, however, so his own sketchbooks, drawings, and writings from the time, together with Daniele Pauly's later essays (1980, 1982) provide close-up accounts of how Le Corbusier did "get all of that." An examination of these accounts of the work on Ronchamp and an assortment of other sources establishes the key role of drawing in design. This role may be stated as the second epistemological property of study drawings: *study drawings provide a graphic means to generate information within the design task.* In the discussion below I will refer to *information* in its general sense as the content of an organized body of knowledge—such as a design task.

4

GRAPHIC PROCESSES[1]

But where did I get all of that?

LE CORBUSIER, upon returning to the hill at Ronchamp several years after the project had been completed

STUDY DRAWINGS
GENERATE INFORMATION

Not all architects agree that design study drawings provide an active means for generating design information; many consider study drawings as records of images previously conceived in the designer's mind. Joseph Esherick wrote, "I do not use drawings 'for thinking' but typically think out what I want to do and then draw it" (pers. com. 1989). Peter Eisenman characterized the drawing practice of other architects by saying: "I think people have images, preconceived images. Most people design with an image in their head; the drawing is a materialization of that visual image." And Le Corbusier viewed drawing as subordinate to mental images: using Ronchamp as one example, he explained that he started a design task by storing and "incubating" data about the project and the site in his memory for some months, but not making any drawings (Pauly 1982, xiv). After the incubation came the "spontaneous birth . . . of the whole work, all at once and all of a sudden" (Pauly 1982, xvi). These are clear statements from respectable sources, but the graphic evidence of their work shows that even such experienced designers may not be infallible observers of their own intentions and processes. I

---

[1]Portions of this chapter have appeared in the *Journal of Architectural Education,* 1992, 46(1): 28-39.

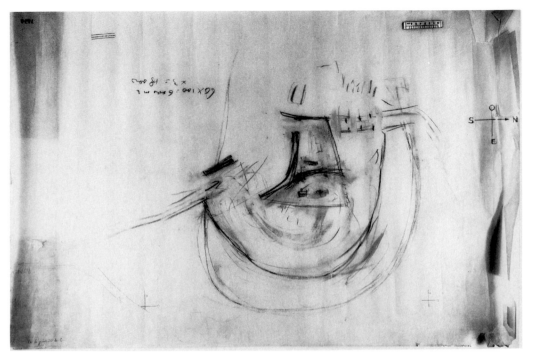

FIGURE 4-1. Le Corbusier: sketch site plan for the chapel at Ronchamp, June 6, 1950. Charcoal and red pencil on heavy tracing paper; 1:200 metric scale (about $\frac{1}{16}'' = 1'$-$0''$ scale). This figure shows the extent of the full drawing page, 1180mm × 750mm (about 46″ × 30″). The centimeter rule on the page is a graphic scale not for the drawing but for the size of the page. © *1922 ARS, N.Y./SPADEM, Paris.*

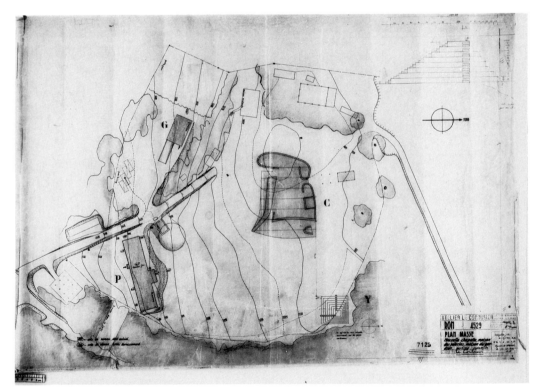

FIGURE 4-2. Le Corbusier: design development drawing of site plan for the chapel at Ronchamp, December 15, 1952. Ink, black and red pencil on heavy tracing paper; 1:200 metric scale. This figure also shows the full drawing page 1080mm × 730mm (about 42″ × 29″). © *1922 ARS, N.Y./SPADEM, Paris.*

will let these architects' drawings speak for themselves on this subject, then, beginning with Le Corbusier's familiar "first" drawing for Ronchamp (figure 4-1).

Le Corbusier first visited the site on Sunday, June 4, 1950. On the following Tuesday, June 6, probably back in his Paris office, he drew the first plan for the chapel. To see whether this drawing is the "whole work, all at once and all of a sudden," compare its major elements

with the almost-final plan (figure 4-2) drawn December 1952—30 months later—when the design development drawings were submitted for approval.

The overall gesture of the first plan clearly persists in the final plan and in the completed building; Le Corbusier never wavered from his first sense that this was to be an expressionistic building of powerful sweeping movements. But there are at least three major differ-

FIGURE 4-3. Le Corbusier: study sketch plan for the chapel at Ronchamp, June 6, 1950. Pencil on heavy tracing paper; same 1:200 scale as the charcoal drawing—presumably an overlay on that drawing. The smaller size of the drawing page, at 660mm × 540mm (about 26″ × 21″), also supports the inference that this is an overlay study. *© 1922 ARS, N.Y./SPADEM, Paris.*

ences in design content between the drawings in figure 4-1 and figure 4-2.

The most conspicuous difference between the drawings is in the form of the north and west walls. In the first plan, Le Corbusier paid most attention to the exterior spaces at the south and east; the interior is almost-undifferentiated leftover space, contained but not formed by the lighter and more tentative lines of the north and west walls. Only later the same day (June 6), in a pencil overlay sketch, did he transform these walls by introducing the half-dome towers that hold and light the three small chapels (figure 4-3). These sketches demonstrate that the three chapels followed as a graphic development from the rudimentary north and west walls of the first sketch.

A second major difference between the early and late drawings is in the character of the south wall. In none of his early drawings did Le Corbusier foresee the dramatic 3.7-meter thickness of the completed building's south wall; the multiple lines of the south wall in the first charcoal sketch were a series of attempts to find the right curve, not a statement of the thick wall—as evidenced by subsequent drawings that show this wall

with a nominal thickness of 1 meter or less (figure 4-3). The remarkable conception of the wall as a volume in itself did not appear for about three and one-half months and did not reach its eventual thickness until more than two years after the first drawing.[2]

A third difference between the drawings concerns the east crescent, a striking part of the first sketch. This crescent evolved over the next two years into a substantial element of site design—an elaborate platformed esplanade, like a half-saucer, intended to contain the entire space for the outdoor audience (figure 4-4). The

[2]The south wall always had graphic emphasis, but the wall grew progressively thicker through schematic design and design development: a drawing dated July 6, 1950, shows it about the same thickness as the other walls. Its first depiction with more than nominal thickness was in a drawing made on October 30, 1950, at a thickness of about 2 meters—a dimension that persisted as late as January 2, 1951. The first drawing showing its eventual thickness of about 3.7 meters is September 9, 1952; that is, 27 months after the first drawing. Apparently the thickness of the south wall was a matter of some disagreement in the office; Maisonnier, Le Corbusier's assistant, kept drawing the wall much thinner than did Le Corbusier. As late as December 3, 1953, Maisonnier's drawing shows the south wall with only a nominal thickness of less than 1 meter.

FIGURE 4-4. Le Corbusier: south elevation of the chapel at Ronchamp drawn by Maisonnier, 195?. Ink on heavy tracing paper. © *1922 ARS, N.Y./SPADEM, Paris.*

esplanade was abandoned in December 1952 (figure 4-2) in favor of two other built elements—the round hill at the southeast corner and the stepped pyramid at the northeast corner that punctuates the ragged tree line—to provide a marked change in the character of the assembly area.[3]

Further evidence of changes between Le Corbusier's early and final thinking about the project can be found at the northwest corner of the building. Shown on the drawing in figure 4-1 is the suggestion of a grid or colonnade continuing the line of the west wall to meet the north access road. This object evolved into a scaffold-like shelter that persisted until the last development drawings and models. Although the shelter is still included on the drawing in figure 4-2, it was dropped from the final construction drawings and was never built.

Thus it seems fair to say that the first charcoal drawing completed on June 6, 1950, contains less—or,

less reliable—information about the final building than did the later drawings, not just in minor developmental details but in major features. The early drawing lacks several significant components that were added later; it includes hints of several other major components that were developed for a while and then rejected; and it shows the building as one part of an elaborate site complex rather than as the freestanding single object that was actually built. These differences suggest a long period of development rather than a spontaneous birth.

Furthermore, there is some doubt that either the charcoal sketch of June 6 or the lost sketches made at the site on June 4 were actually the first drawings for the project. In one of his sketchbooks Le Corbusier made two earlier drawings of the hill at Ronchamp. One of these drawings clearly shows the ruins of the existing chapel; the other, labeled "The Chapel of Ronchamp," might be either the existing chapel seen from another angle or an idea for the new chapel (figure 4-5). Françoise de Franclieu, annotator of the published sketchbooks, opts for the latter:

> [This drawing is] the first sketch for Ronchamp when Le Corbusier "took possession" of the site as he saw it from the Paris-Basel train May 20, 1950, and before he had actually visited the site on June 4. He felt immediately in harmony with this space open at all points with the horizon and then and

[3]The drawing in figure 4-2 is one of two alternative plans of the same date. One plan (figure 4-2) shows the stepped pyramid and round hill bracketing the east congregation area; the other plan (not reproduced here) shows the crescent form developed into the raised esplanade. It seems clear that these drawings present the two versions of the assembly area as alternatives. I find no record of the evaluation of these drawings, but Pauly (1980, 57) notes that Le Corbusier had come under heavy criticism for cost estimates that exceeded the owner's budget. The esplanade was certainly a very costly element and so a probable candidate for elimination.

there drew the basic silhouette of what would become the chapel of Notre Dame du Haupt (De Franclieu 1981, 2-23).

De Franclieu was convinced that the sketch was not a changed view of the hill but a quick note of an idea for the new building.[4] Yet, like the charcoal plan of June 6, this quick note cannot qualify as a full description of the work.

The graphic evidence of his completed drawings casts some doubt, then, not only on Le Corbusier's "spontaneous birth" account of his working process, but also on his claim of setting out the "whole work, all at once and all of a sudden." And the evidence of the completed drawings is confirmed by any plausible version of what Le Corbusier could have had in mind as he drew them: it is hard to believe, for instance, that when Le Corbusier made the charcoal drawing in his office on June 6 he had a mental image of the three small chapels but thought it unimportant to draw them; or that he thought it important but was unable to do it; or that on any of the plans he drew that day he knew what the site development or the building interior ought to be but could not get it right on the drawing. Like other architects, he drew—he could only have drawn—as much as he knew at that moment, constructing the drawing one step at a time, with his own response to each drawing stroke calling up the next stroke. The sequence of stroke/response/stroke constitutes an iterative drawing cycle, not just from one drawing to another, but stroke by stroke anywhere within any drawing; it is the fundamental act in the working process of design.

To illustrate how this drawing cycle generates design information, consider a detailed example focusing on just the central part of Le Corbusier's charcoal drawing (that is, just the plan of the main building), shown at the actual size he drew it (figure 4-6).

Some background will be necessary to set the scene for Le Corbusier's work on the drawing: as he later wrote, for several months before he first visited Ronchamp he had been gathering information about the project and thinking about the site and program (Pauly 1982, xviii). And, according to Pauly, Le Corbusier had had a

FIGURE 4-5. Le Corbusier: sketch of the hill at Ronchamp, drawn from the Paris-Basel train, May 20, 1950. Ink on 4″ × 6″ page of sketchbook. *From The Le Corbusier Sketchbooks, vol. 2. Copyright: Architectural History Foundation and MIT Press. Sketchbook #D-17, Reproduced by permission of MIT Press.*

strong reaction to the spaces of the site when he visited it on June 4. At that visit he had almost certainly formed some mental image of concave shapes to contain the south entry space and the east assembly space: Pauly writes that Le Corbusier had made a (probably single-line) notebook plan of the south and east walls while he was there.[5] Two days later, in his Paris office, Le Corbusier had tacked down a large sheet of tracing paper, probably over a surveyor's base plan of the site. The base plan was oriented with north to the right (i.e., *east down*).[6] The base plan would likely have shown

---

[4]Pauly (1980, 33) suggests that both of the sketches made from the train on May 20 were views of the ruins of the previous chapel. But Le Corbusier (1960, 166) includes this sketch among other early sketches of the chapel; it seems unlikely that he would, without special comment, so include a sketch of the previous building.

[5]Pauly (1980, 34) quotes a description by Chanoine Ledeur (a member of the building committee), who says that he was standing next to Le Corbusier on the hill at Ronchamp on Sunday, June 4: "I saw his immediate reaction to the site, the first pencil stroke of the drawing: the south wall, he did *this* (tracing a concave line with a gesture in the air). Then it was necessary to group the pilgrims in front of the wall where he placed the altar, whose curve responded to that of the south wall: next it was only necessary to join the two curves" (Pauly's parentheses; translated by author). Ledeur's description does not mention the north and west walls, but it otherwise supports Pauly's assertion that Le Corbusier transcribed his charcoal sketch of June 6 from an earlier sketchbook drawing made at the site.

[6]*East down* because that is the way Le Corbusier reproduced the drawing in his own book (1957, 89). Both the *Le Corbusier Archive* (on p. 158) and Pauly's article (1982, xxiii) reverse the drawing on the book page (i.e., *east up*) from the architect's own layout. The *east down* orientation probably implies Le Corbusier's psychological point of view: looking toward the building as one of the pilgrims facing the building, rather than out from the building as an owner or cleric viewing the congregation.

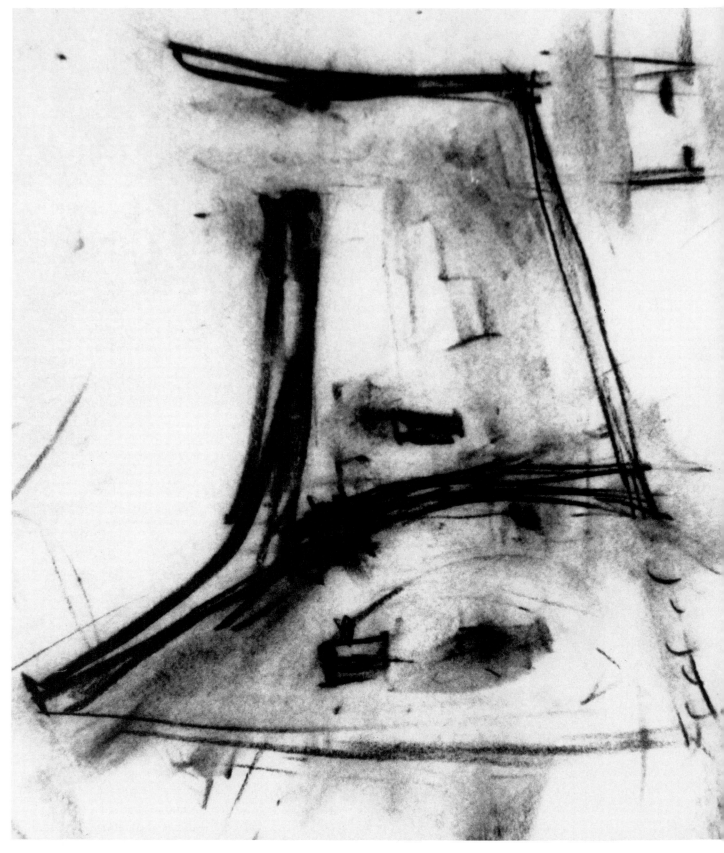

FIGURE 4-6. Le Corbusier: sketch site plan for the chapel at Ronchamp, June 6, 1950. Detail of central part of the drawing from figure 4-1, shown here about actual size. © *1922 ARS, N.Y./SPADEM, Paris.*

contours, trees, the existing building, and the access roads.

Pauly (1980, 34) supplies a detailed account of how Le Corbusier drew the plan: "with four lines the architect *finds* the plan of the chapel . . . two curved lines, one toward the south, the other toward the east, . . . toward the open country; the space between the convexity of these two lines is closed by two straight lines meeting at an obtuse angle . . ." (Pauly's emphasis).

If Pauly is right in believing that the charcoal drawing began as a straightforward transcription of a (single-line) notebook sketch, Le Corbusier probably could have drawn out the south and east walls of the plan straightaway and followed them immediately with the north and west walls, using all neat double lines (figure 4-7) such as those that still show for the north and west walls (figure 4-6). These lines do express a general idea of the project as it was later developed, but this view of everything-done-in-four-quick-lines does not fit all the facts on the page. None of the four lines is a single stroke, for example; the south wall has at least six strokes, the east wall at least four, the west and north at least two each. Furthermore, all the lines show graphic evidence of the changes Le Corbusier made as the drawing took shape: the false starts and modifications, the graphic experiments, rubbings-out, redrawings, and additions. Such changes could have been made either by backtracking to revise each line as he made it or, more likely, by drawing all four lines as a transcription and development from the lines in the sketchbook and then changing things that dissatisfied him, first at one place and then at another. Whichever way he started, and even if he had a notion of concave site spaces, his subsequent steps were not records of a preconceived mental picture of the building, but responses to the evolving graphic image, with each stroke triggering each next stroke (or erasure) to make the completed drawing shown in the figure.[7]

An example in still finer detail in the area of the east wall almost shows the sequence of individual strokes (figure 4-8): here in this now-frozen scenario is evidence that Le Corbusier returned to try—one after another—four alternative arcs for the east wall to meet the north wall at various angles. He tested several lengths

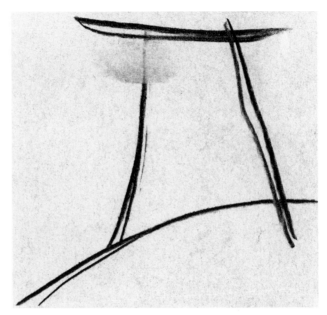

FIGURE 4-7. Author (after Le Corbusier). Medium soft charcoal on heavy tracing paper, shown here at about 40 percent of actual size. The drawing shows Pauly's hypothetical "first four lines" of figure 4-6, made into double lines as Le Corbusier might have done before he started modifications. Pauly says that Le Corbusier drew the south and east lines first as transcriptions from an earlier (single-line) sketch made at the site; the observations below suggest otherwise and demonstrate that even transcription involves a substantial amount of graphic interpretation. *My observations from having tried to reconstruct the first step in Le Corbusier's drawing: (1) The east line was drawn first, starting as a double line but merging into one; (2) the west line was drawn next (note that it is an arc opposing the east line, not a straight line paired with the north lines, as Pauly says); (3) the lines of the south wall were drawn from bottom to top, then erased with a fingertip to open up the entrance; (4) the north wall was drawn last, from top to bottom; it is difficult for right-handed persons such as Le Corbusier and me to make straight parallel freehand lines in this position; (5) knowing what we do about the finished building, the whole plan may also be read as a (vertical) transverse section of the whole building; the west wall especially invites reading as the characteristic Ronchamp roof section as shown in figure 6-3. Courtesy Daniel Herbert after Le Corbusier, © 1922 ARS, N.Y./SPADEM, Paris.*

for the extended end of the north wall. He drew and rubbed out several attempts to connect the two curves at the southeast corner, but the drawing had by then become too smudged to allow further efforts and he left that area unresolved for exploration on subsequent overlay drawings that still did not reach a conclusion. These explorations can only be read as cycles of graphic experiments: Le Corbusier making one stroke, or mark, and then interpreting it—that is, evaluating the mark in its graphic context, and reevaluating the whole graphic context as affected by the new mark—to see what to do next. Such a step-by-step progression explains why Le

---

[7]Pauly (1980, 39) also notes that Le Corbusier's work developed through drawing rather than by separate mental composition: "the mark searches out the idea . . ." and "the idea is born at the same time as the mark . . ." (translated by author).

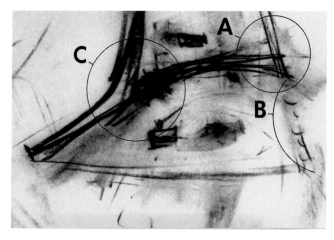

FIGURE 4-8. Le Corbusier: the chapel at Ronchamp; detail of central part of June 6, 1950, sketch plan, east wall (shown here about 40 percent of actual size). Area "A" shows three different attempts to find the proper angle of intersection; the middle line, with its slightly acute angle, is close to the final position. Area "B" shows three or four speculative endpoints for the extended north wall beyond the chosen simple intersection; since these show no erasures, they were probably experimental marks to see if the wall ought to be extended. Area "C" shows the unresolved southeast intersection; even the next sketch (figure 4-3) did not resolve this intersection with the same assurance as the southwest intersection and entrance. © *1922 ARS, N.Y./SPADEM, Paris.*

Corbusier drew the three chapels later, after having made the first drawing without them: he was dissatisfied with what he saw in his earlier drawing and he made a new one to improve it.[8] Through cycles of drawing and interpretation, then, not just from one drawing to another but within each drawing, Le Corbusier developed the implications of his first sketch in a complex graphic discourse that produced the now-familiar building.

The point of the analysis in this scenario is not to discover the "real" starting point and sequence of this drawing, but to establish the existence of a short-term elemental drawing cycle of *mark/interpretation/mark,* etc., where the act of making each mark renews, expands, and redefines the conceptual scope of the design task in progressive responses to the evolving composition on the drawing page.

Thus both evidence and inference show that, contrary to his own statement, Le Corbusier used his study drawings not as a medium for recording already conceived mental images but as active participants in his thinking. He used them, in short, to generate new information within the design task. It does not diminish either the architect or the building to find that the design for Ronchamp developed over a substantial time through a series of drawings, each with its own internal evolution.

Such an evolution is whole and sudden enough for most purposes, but not for purposes of understanding the role of drawing in design. Other designers ought not to be misled in understanding their own work by Le Corbusier's fallible version of how he went about his.

The point at issue here is what designers can learn about the role of drawings in the working processes of design, so it is essential to recognize that the design for Ronchamp was not the sudden birth and recording of an already conceived image but the outcome of an extended development proceeding graphically. It is also essential to recognize that this development takes place not just in abrupt leaps from one drawing to another but in incremental, moment-by-moment cycles of marks and interpretations within each drawing.

Can this analysis of graphic development apply to Joseph Esherick's statement that he does not use drawings for thinking, but imagines what he wants to do and then draws it? Consider the following excerpts from the interview with Esherick:

> **DH:** How close is this drawing to what you woke up in the morning thinking you were going to draw?
>
> **JE:** It isn't very close because the original idea of what I was going to do was to not go back here to get in but to bring the pathway through somehow in here; then I noticed on the drawing underneath, that would wipe out those trees.
>
> **DH:** There were facts shown on the earlier drawing that your solution conflicted with?
>
> **JE:** Yes, I was not focusing on the trees, there are so many trees you can't remember where all of them are; so I wasn't sure whether those trees were in existence or not.

---

[8]Pauly (1982, xviii) convincingly traces the possible sources of the images for the chapels back through Le Corbusier's earlier sketchbooks, but my point here is that these images were brought into the design task through the graphic discourse of the study drawings, not conceived previously in the architect's mind for this project. This is certain because he did not include them in his first drawing.

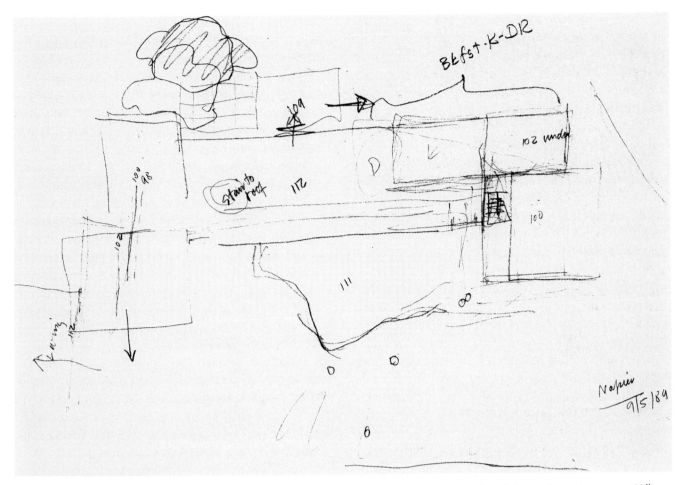

FIGURE 4-9. Joseph Esherick: site study for house in rural California, September 5, 1989. Pencil on lightweight tracing paper; 22″ × 14″. *Courtesy Joseph Esherick.*

. . . .

. . . I was trying to challenge the basic idea; if it isn't a good idea, it ought to change. I sort of arbitrarily see what the consequences of changing it are.

DH: You want to see if it can be violated and you use the drawing to find out.

JE: Yes.

. . . .

(talking as he draws—figure 4-9) . . . And we do need some small interior stair . . . maybe back here at the corner of the garage . . . strictly a service stair that takes you down to the garage and these things that're under . . . and then these are . . . directed somehow along here. . . .

DH: (referring to the above drawing) This drawing you just did "on-line" took eight or nine minutes or so as you talked it through. . . . Suppose you had made it on your own, would you guess it would take about that same amount of time, a little less or a little more? Or did talking it through disturb the process?

JE: Maybe a little less. Talking it through really didn't disturb the process because I would be questioning myself in exactly the same way. I would be explaining to myself all the things I was doing just now.

In practice, then, it appears the Esherick makes study drawings in about the same way that Le Corbusier did: through complex real-time cycles of drawing/interpretation/drawing/etc., using the act of drawing to explore, to test, to generate new information within the design task. Material from my interviews with Stern, Tigerman, and Jahn, as well as evidence from their drawings, confirms that for them such use of study drawings is the rule rather than the exception. Indeed, the ambiguous, unfinished appearance of most study drawings is more readily explained by regarding them as exploratory instruments rather than as records of complete images separately conceived in the mind of the designer.

And what of Eisenman's assertion that most designers have preconceived visual images in their head and that their drawings are a materialization of those images? Eisenman was only partly correct: the evidence above shows that other designers may indeed have some mental image, or perhaps a kinesthetic or emotional feeling that they do intend to realize; but the image or feeling turns out not to be as clear or as complete as they (or Eisenman) think it is, so they are forced to explore it through graphic manipulation, learning as they go by reinterpreting the drawing in the light of each new mark as it is made. Through this manipulation most designers find things of which they had no mental image when they began to draw; they generate information through their use of the graphic medium.

UNCERTAINTY IN DESIGN STUDY DRAWINGS

Every feeling waits upon its gesture. Then when it does come, how unpredictable it turns out to be. . . .

EUDORA WELTY, *One Time, One Place*

The business of reinterpreting each mark as it is made and thereby finding new information means that the design task as a whole is uncertain. This built-in uncertainty of the whole task derives from the uncertainty of each incremental step. A drawing takes real time, and each mark as it is made immediately becomes a new element that expands and redefines the design task. For example, Le Corbusier's broad sweeping gestures that characterize the final design of Ronchamp were not themselves preconceived entities and were not recorded all at once; the charcoal traces of his gestures were marks of new information that could have emerged only through the physical act of drawing.

Thus each mark requires the designer to make a new interpretation of all past marks, an interpretation that cannot be resolved so long as there is the expectation of some next mark. And, since each new mark is made in response to a previous interpretation, each mark becomes a new, unpredictable influence on every next mark. Situating each newly made current mark between an unresolved past and an unpredictable future means that the information generated by the drawing is not only new but contingent; that is, dependent for its existence on something not yet certain.

This built-in contingency of study drawings does not exhaust the possibilities for uncertainty within the design task, however; the designer can deliberately introduce uncertainty by choosing a suitable drawing strategy.

DRAWING STRATEGIES

The matter of deliberately choosing a drawing strategy to open the way for uncertainty was raised by Eisenman in the comment noted in chapter 2 concerning drawing as a design issue (repeated and extended below). After having described other architects' drawing as a way to materialize preconceived visual images, Eisenman contrasted his approach:

> Now, I don't draw that way. . . . What I do is set up a series of ideas or rules or strategies and draw into [them] . . . trying to find some form in those ideas. In other words, my drawings are rather more haptic or circumstantial and in them I find things that I wouldn't have found if I had said "This is what I want" to start with. I find things that I might never have designed because there's no preconception in the drawing, there's no ideation that has visual image attached to it. I think that's a big difference from most architects.

Eisenman was more correct this time in finding a difference between his strategic approach to drawing and that of most other designers. Where he sets out expressly to employ the medium as a substantial and even separate design issue, most other architects just draw, tacitly assuming that the graphic skills they learned through education and practice will enable them to represent directly whatever is important to the content of the design task. Because almost any kind of study drawing induces circumstantial discoveries and generates contingent information that the designer could not have conceived originally, these two strategic approaches—Eisenman's and others'—appear to converge to a similar result. The convergence is more apparent than real, however, because the approach of tacitly assuming a drawing strategy differs from that of expressly choosing one. Examples of these two strategic approaches will illustrate the difference.

I will return again to Le Corbusier's charcoal drawing of June 6—this time as a basis for conjecture about his strategic approach to drawing. When Le Corbusier reached for charcoal and a large sheet of tracing paper, he chose materials that encouraged free arm and hand movements (the main figure on the page is about 20 inches across), materials that invited—or even demanded—the sweeping gestures of the drawing. Charcoal allowed Le Corbusier the wide range of line weights noted above, and permitted him to rub out and smudge lines directly with a finger, without breaking his concentration to pick up another tool. His use of charcoal discouraged fine finger movements; he could not have used charcoal if he had intended to trace the lines of the existing ruins as a basis for the new building or if he were drawing in a pocket sketchbook. The drawing shows Le Corbusier's tacit, intuitive assumption of a graphic strategy. If this strategy were formulated as an explicit ideological statement about the role of graphics in design, it might read as follows: *Graphic traces of arm/hand kinesthetic gestures responding expressively to program and site may be read directly as representations of appropriate architectural forms.*

Describing a very dissimilar approach to the role of graphics in design, Eisenman commented about one of his parti[9] drawings for the Design, Architecture, Art and Planning (DAAP) project at the University of Cincinnati (figure 4-10):

> I don't think it's mathematical, it's some way . . . to find an order in the arbitrary curving, but it's not mathematical, it's a kind of geometric progression, asymptotical. Mathematical is too narrative. I'm always looking for the necessary logic of these arbitrary things, their own logic . . . which may be illogical.

[9]A *parti* is an architectural drawing that shows only the basic idea or schematic organization for a design.

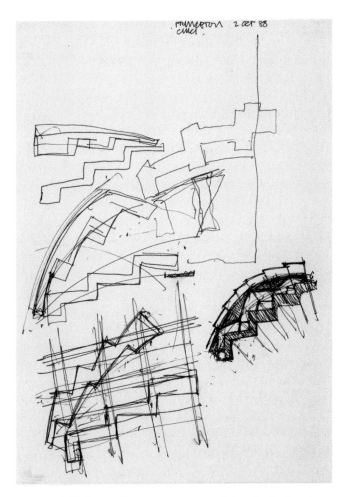

FIGURE 4-10. Peter Eisenman: conceptual sketch plan for the College of Design, Architecture, Art and Planning (DAAP), University of Cinicinnati, October 2, 1988. Ink on lightweight yellow tracing paper from a bound pad, 8½″ × 11″. The drawing shows the segmented curve as an addition to an existing "chevron" building complex; the existing building is abstracted and made more regular than its actual plan. The partly hatched drawing (right central) is a key drawing of which Eisenman said: ". . . that's where I started to think about the line as segmented. I think that's where it becomes interesting." The curve's segments are derived radially from the abstracted and idealized vertices of the chevron. *Courtesy Peter Eisenman.*

If this statement were formulated as an ideological statement to provide a basis for comparison with the statement contrived above to represent Le Corbusier's strategy, it might read as follows: *Drawings representing formal hypotheses based on program and site issues are graphic artifacts; artificial graphic manipulation of these lines is required to generate architectural form; "appropriateness" is moot.*

These two formulations offer unlike approaches to the larger issues of design as well as to the role of graphic media, but the point in formulating and comparing the statements here is neither to judge one approach to design as ideologically better than the other nor to determine a fixed meaning of Le Corbusier's and Eisenman's drawings.[10] Rather, the point is to focus narrowly on graphic processes—to understand the differences between *tacitly assuming* a strategic approach to drawing and *explicitly choosing* one.

There are two such differences: first, approaching a drawing strategy as an explicit choice makes the designer responsible for more of what happens throughout the entire design process than does the tacit assumption; and second, the explicit choice requires more decisions about architectural form within the design task than does the tacit assumption. In the examples above, Le Corbusier dealt with program, site conditions, and technology as foreground issues, while Eisenman dealt with program, site conditions, technology, and *media* as foreground issues in reaching decisions about architectural form. Furthermore, the explicit strategy stated here (although it is not the only possible explicit strategy) treats drawing not just as another foreground issue but as one that is prior to all other issues in that it gives them order and meaning. Conversely, the tacit assumption of a drawing strategy—that is, without explicit formulation—treats drawing as a part of the background; a neutral, transparent medium that allows the designer directly to engage real objects and spaces that are considered to make up the design task.

It should be apparent through this discussion, however, that study drawings are not neutral; they are not transparent representations of a separate objective reality conceived beforehand by the designer. On the contrary, they are an imposed order that introduces substantial new issues into the design task—issues that

have significant effects. The act of drawing introduces new issues because the new information generated within the design task is *graphic* information. Such graphic information takes on the peculiar characteristics of both the physical medium and the drawing strategy; that is, it has its own idiom, as shown by the examples of both Le Corbusier's large charcoal drawings and Eisenman's small pen-and-ink sketches. Furthermore, these idiomatic effects are introduced whether or not the designer acknowledges them. The designer cannot choose to work in such a way that media have no effect. Although the designer can decline to formulate an explicit foreground drawing strategy, this default choice does not remove the effects of the medium on the design task; it only removes them from the list of issues for which the designer agrees to be responsible. Thus the contrast between tacit assumption and explicit formulation has to do with the extent of the designer's responsibility for the working process and for the breadth of issues that will contribute to architectural form.

DRAWING STRATEGIES AS A SOURCE OF UNCERTAINTY

Responsibility for the process does not necessarily imply control of the information generated, however, because one could choose a drawing (or design) strategy that deliberately disrupts control by imposing a fixed order. Eisenman described how the strategy worked for the DAAP project (figure 4-10): once he had formulated this order and laid out its geometry, everyone involved in the working process understood that it was to be given first consideration in making design decisions. The fixed order governed the location and form of structural members, partitions, openings, and ceiling modulations. Its rules required, for example, that columns be placed at the radial lines, and that each space change at least one of its dimensions at a radial line. Applying such rules could produce a cascade of secondary effects: a geometrically proposed column location could influence the width of an exit stairway required by the building code, or a difference in ceiling height could change the size of overhead beams. In use, such arbitrary ordering becomes almost an *algorithm*—that is, a rigorously specified procedure—for generating form.

---

[10]The two ideological approaches toward drawing formulated here—the intuitive gesture and the rational manipulation—are not peculiar to Le Corbusier or to Eisenman, and are not even consistently adopted throughout their own work: Eisenman uses different drawing strategies on different projects. He also uses a different drawing strategy in the early (conceptual) stages of his work than in the later (developmental) stages; his first sketches for the DAAP project are exactly the same kind of intuitive gesture that Le Corbusier used for Ronchamp, except that Eisenman (he says) is searching for a geometric basis that will generate form and Le Corbusier apparently is searching directly for form. And Le Corbusier's *Modulor* is clearly an effort to use rational manipulation as a basis for generating form. See also Papadakis, Cooke, and Benjamin (1989) for descriptions by Bernard Tschumi and Daniel Libeskind of geometric generators in their work.

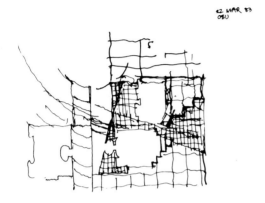

FIGURE 4-11. Peter Eisenman: conceptual sketch plan, Wexner Center for the Visual Arts, Ohio State University, Columbus, Ohio, March 22, 1983. Ink on heavy white tracing paper from bound pad; 8½″ × 11″. *Courtesy Peter Eisenman.*

Eisenman and several other contemporary architects[11] have employed various algorithmic strategies for generating form, making the graphic processes a foreground issue rather than a background issue and thereby challenging the tacit assumption that certainty and subjectively determined unity are intrinsic architectural values.

Besides imposing his handmade graphic algorithms that challenge certainty—such as in the DAAP project—Eisenman has also suggested a related role for computers in design:

> The computer can do things that the human mind can conceptualize but not visualize; it does things that you would never be able to draw, and therefore it produces things that, when you build them, clearly are not in the control of the creative subject. And I have always been interested [in removing] the creative subject from the work as

far as possible, that is, to diminish the creative subject: me. Even though I am still present.

Eisenman used the computer in just this role in his 1987 competition entry for the Biological Research Facility for the University of Frankfurt, Germany (Yessios, 1987).

Such efforts to introduce uncertainty with a systematic, seemingly *certain* algorithmic process—either by hand or by computer—are not the anomalies they might seem: even an elementary geometric process like superimposing two differently oriented rectangular coordinate systems within a building plan, as Eisenman does in the Wexner Center at Ohio State University (figure 4-11), produces uncertain, unpredictable events in the hurly-burly of the design task. The collisions between coordinate systems inevitably generate not only unpredictable forms and spaces but unpredictable impacts on program, site-related, and technological elements. More complex multi-step algorithms, such as those that Eisenman and Bernard Tschumi have developed for modular transformations,[12] are unpredictable in any architectural sense of the word. Yet the human designer does not disappear: even the most rigorous algorithmic process necessarily has a subjective content, not only because any such process is itself necessarily a human artifact but also because its use reflects a human choice among artifacts—the selection of a particular geometry or a specific program.

BEYOND "I'S" AND MAN

Eisenman's observation proposes that computers might become a means of diminishing the presence of the creative subject. This interest in transcending the "I" of Le Corbusier's question *"Where did I get all of that?"* is not confined to Eisenman or to any particular design approach. Joseph Esherick raised an analogous point in discussing his study drawing elevation for a residence (figure 4-12):

> **DH:** This drawing [you have said shows the use of] factory sash. . . . Where did that contrast come from, that tension between the formal building and the factory sash?

[11]See Eisenman (1989, *P/A*, 92-93) and Papadakis, Cooke, and Benjamin (1989).

[12]Eisenman 1989, *P/A*, 92-93; Tschumi 1989, 175.

FIGURE 4-12. Joseph Esherick: elevation sketch for house, San Francisco, February 25, 1987. Pencil on lightweight yellow sketch paper; about 19″ × 18″, scale ¼ = 1′-0″. *Courtesy Joseph Esherick.*

JE: I don't know where it came from, but I never like to be so consistent that everything follows in a predictable way; it seems to me that life isn't like that. As an idea it may come from reading E.M. Forster, who was a master at the art of suggesting where the predictable world is and then, all of a sudden, *bang!,* it's someplace else again. In all of Forster's novels — *A Passage to India, Howard's End* — there's always that traumatic experience. There's one where an English woman and an Italian man marry and have a baby and are riding in a carriage that overturns and the baby is killed. In one little paragraph, such a cataclysmic event! The possibility of multiple interpretations has always . . . [pause] . . . it doesn't seem to me that being totally predictable and consistent is what you want to do.

Similarly, Stern explained the beginning of his project for the U.S. Embassy annex in Budapest (figure 4-13):

This is the way I work sometimes: this is a xerox, put together from some buildings by Lutyens. I xeroxed them and cut them apart to make an armature for the first notion of this building. I drew over the Lutyens building and then I started to make some notes about the consular function and the office building and [etc.]. . . ."

Both Esherick and Stern have deliberately introduced devices to extend the design task, although not in the same way. Stern's photocopy provided a graphic framework that allowed him to leap into the middle of the drawing sequence, giving even his first marks a full graphic context from an outside source. Although Esherick's device was more a philosophical reflection than a strictly graphic notion, it had to be expressed by drawing to become a part of the design task. Stanley Tigerman's fantasy and reflection sketches (figure 4-14) also may be seen as excursions outside the confines of any one design process, just like many of Le Corbusier's notebook sketches and Jahn's analytical drawing (figure 4-15). This latter group of devices differs from Eisenman's explicit formulation and systematic exploitation of the geometric algorithm as a design issue; nevertheless, these devices confirm a common need to take deliberate steps to overcome the limitations of individual experience, to go beyond the particulars of any one commission or any given formulation of program and context statements. Moreover, since all these devices eventually involve expression in graphic media, they become subject to the effects and the mark/interpretation/mark cycle as the graphic composition develops on the page.

Thus it appears that study drawings may have two kinds of uncertainty; built-in and deliberate. Built-in uncertainty, derived from the situation of each current mark between an unresolved past and an unpredictable future, is the source of study drawing's endless contingency. Deliberately sought uncertainty reaches outside the culturally determined constraints of the design task, and, as Esherick suggests, outside the possibility of predictability as a condition of human experience.

UNCERTAINTY AND INTERPRETATION

The observations concerning graphics as a source of uncertainty provide a new basis for understanding how the mark/interpretation/mark cycle works within

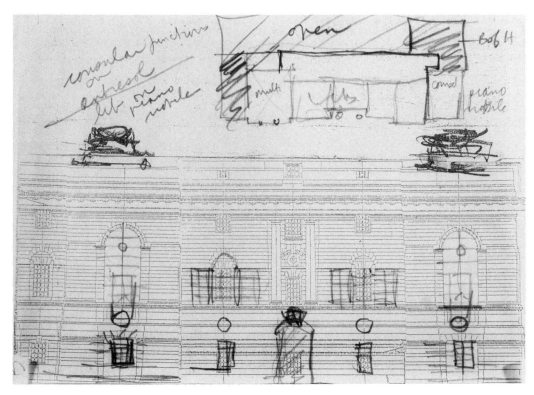

FIGURE 4-13. Robert Stern: conceptual sketch elevation (below) and plan (above), U.S. Embassy annex, Budapest, Hungary, May 1989. Marking pen on a photocopy print; 8½″ × 11″. *Courtesy Robert A.M. Stern Architects.*

the design task. The earlier discussion suggested that the drawing cycle involved the designer's evaluating the mark in its graphic context, and then reevaluating the whole graphic context as affected by the uncertainty of the new mark. This description implies that in the mark/interpretation/mark cycle it is only the *mark* member of the cycle that is uncertain. But the cycle is richer and more complex than that; in fact, the *interpretation* member of the cycle is also uncertain, as literary critic Stanley Fish points out in describing the reader's interpretive activities in literature:

> The reader's activities . . . include the making and revising of assumptions, the rendering and regretting of judgments, the coming to and abandoning of conclusions, the giving and withdrawing of approval, the specifying of causes, the asking of questions, the supplying of answers, the solving of puzzles. In a word, these activities are interpretive . . . [they may be described as] a moving field of concerns, at once wholly present (not waiting for meaning but constituting meaning) and continually in the act of reconstituting itself." (Fish 1980, 158-59; Fish's parentheses).

Fish's description of the reader's "moving field of concerns . . . continually . . . reconstituting itself" can be applied directly to the design task; this is exactly the contingent role of both the mark and its interpretation in the mark/interpretation/mark cycle. Although Fish describes only the reader's activity, the designer acts as both writer and reader—making the mark and simultaneously interpreting it as the basis for the next mark. Learning to design requires learning to read one's own graphic images in this way, as a *moving field of concerns, continually reconstituting itself,* rather than expecting the drawing to provide a single, complete meaning, simple and certain. Learning to design also requires learning to risk—and even seek—uncertainty by making marks whose meaning will emerge only in the existential act of making them.

So far the discussion has noted that the role of design synthesis drawings is not primarily to record images of an objective reality conceived in the designer's mind, but to provide a graphic means of generating new and always uncertain information within the design task. If design synthesis study drawings include these uncertainties as they generate information, can the same be said for analytic study drawings? Do they

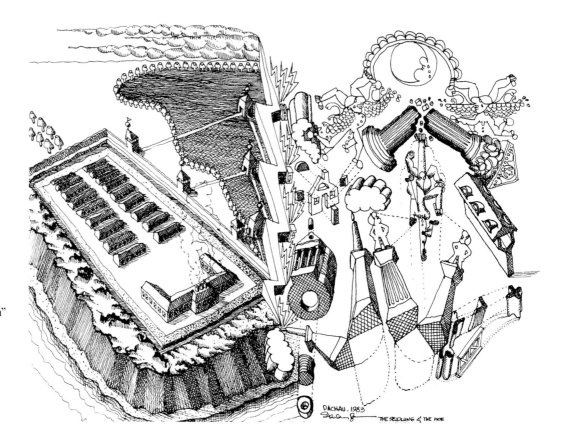

FIGURE 4-14. Stanley Tigerman: (upper) fantasy drawing; (lower) "reflection" drawings. Tigerman's "reflections" are graphic responses to experience— here, from his visit to Dachau, drawn en route from London to Chicago, 1983. *Courtesy Tigerman McCurry Architects.*

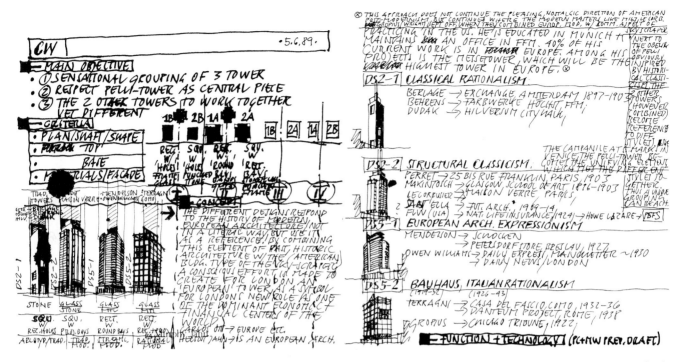

FIGURE 4-15. Helmut Jahn: analytic conceptual sketch, May 6, 1989. Two drawing pages mounted together on one album page. Sepia and black ink on bond paper; 8½″ × 8½″. Jahn called this pair of drawings a graphic "History of Modern European Architecture." *Courtesy Helmut Jahn.*

generate information? Do analytic study drawings also introduce uncertainty?

APPLICATION TO ANALYTIC STUDY DRAWINGS

Chapter 3 established that analytic study drawings such as White's adjacency matrix and diagrams are subject to the same rules of abstraction and information loss as design synthesis drawings. In the light of the discussion above, now it is possible to find further parallels between design synthesis drawings and analytic study drawings: analytic drawings are also deliberate drawing devices with the power to generate information and introduce uncertainty. I will use White's simplified example of the adjacency matrix and diagrams (figure 3-5) again as a subject for analysis.

The matrix (figure 3-5, *left*) forces the designer to identify certain spaces and address certain questions about their relationships. Thus the matrix directly generates a certain kind of information about adjacencies: systematic, limited, and focused by the fixed geometry.

The matrix also offers other means of gaining information: White (1986) notes that one can make "obser-

vations" about the graphic patterns that show up in the matrix. An example might be the cluster of connections noted in the *bathroom* column in the diagram. Based on this cluster, the designer can put this room's "bubble" in the middle of the adjacency diagram and eventually put the room itself in the middle of the house; this observation generates information by making inferences from the overall graphic pattern of the diagram, reading more out of the diagram than was put into it. Another such gain of information, read directly from the graphic pattern of the matrix, White suggests, would be for a matrix (not shown here) that lacked dense clusters of "very important" adjacencies in the matrix; the designer would know that adjacency was not crucial for that project and that other factors—solar orientation, for example—might have a somewhat stronger influence on the plan organization.

On the basis of its geometry, the matrix might appear to be a deliberate device to introduce uncertainty—the matrix might work as Eisenman's algorithm does when it forces its geometry into the design synthesis of the DAAP project. The similarity is only nominal, however: where Eisenman's graphic strategy purposely forces the designers to acknowledge both the presence and the arbitrariness of the graphic medium within the design

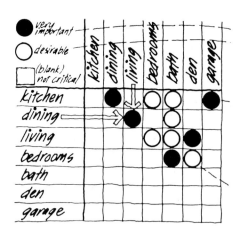 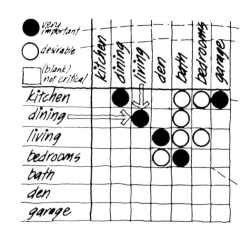

FIGURE 4-16. Graphic accident in an analytic diagram. (Left) repeat of matrix from figure 3-5. (Right) revision of matrix by author), switching *bedrooms* and *den* in column headings. *Courtesy Edward T. White.*

task, the adjacency matrix tacitly invites its user to consider its structure as a transparent and neutral description of objectively real spaces and relationships. By using familiar names for spaces and by concentrating on circulation paths, the matrix reduces the design task's uncertainty even as it adds information about relationships.

The matrix does provide a loose kind of uncertainty, however, by means of graphic accidents. Such an accident could occur, for example, if the column headings of the *bedrooms* and *den* had been switched; then the matrix would have shown a striking gestalt pattern of four heavy dots in a diagonal row (figure 4-16), inviting some kind of response from the designer—perhaps to arrange those rooms along a linear "spine" in the design synthesis drawings. In a similar vein, White brings up another source of what he calls "accidental discoveries":

> Although each analytic routine has a specific purpose and goal and is used to produce information about particular types of project requirements, much of the value of investing in analysis comes from accidental discoveries and unrelated but valuable ideas that occur to us during analysis. While analyzing the project site, ideas may come to mind about energy conservation or about housing the client's operation. (1986, 17)

Uncertainties from accidental discoveries could arise in any analytic procedure; they are less deliberate than Esherick's and Stern's devices and less rigorous than Eisenman's or Tschumi's algorithmic procedures.

Adjacency diagrams (figure 3-5, *middle*) differ from the matrix in their capacity to add information as well as their power to extend the design task. The relationship of bubbles in the adjacency diagram transforms information from matrix to a spatial organization. Even allowing for White's note that this is only a simplified demonstration diagram, this transformation is not as straightforward as it seems. The transformation from the matrix to the adjacency diagram forms a new structure that necessarily incorporates more than just the information from the matrix. The transformed diagram now includes a good many graphic and "house" conventions: that adjacency diagrams ought to avoid crossed circulation paths, that a bathroom does not need an outside view but a kitchen does, that some rooms are bigger than others, etc.; and it also includes an implied grouping that leads to the "zoning" diagram (figure 3-5, *right*).

The zoning diagram makes the addition of the "public" and "private" loops in the diagram appear as natural consequences of the adjacencies given in the adjacency diagram. Yet zoning diagrams, like adjacency diagrams, are not as straightforward as they appear. Including the *garage* as a "private" space, for example, appears to have occurred because of its position below and to the left of the *kitchen* in the adjacency diagram; this position suggested its inclusion in a group with *bedrooms* and *den,* rather than, say, a position above the kitchen in the diagram that would have satisfied the adjacency matrix just as well but would have suggested its inclusion in the "public" group of *kitchen, dining,* and *living.* Since the garage bubble must be shown somewhere, its actual position may be either another kind of graphic accident, a hidden preference of the designer, or a tacit assumption from the cultural background of the design task.

To the extent that these simplified matrix, adjacency, and zoning diagrams represent analytic study drawings, it seems that they do help to generate information within the design task. At least they force the designer to address certain issues, they prompt certain kinds of responses, and they record the information they elicit. Within their sphere, matrices and adjacency diagrams make the designer's working process more precise.

Yet only indirectly and by accident do analytic drawings extend the design task beyond its customary limits. The insistent mechanics of analytic drawings and their routines tend to conceal their limited range. White (1986, 17) warns that designers must stay in control of these routines because "... they seem ... only to require us to perform the prescribed steps of the process and wait patiently for the results."

White's warning recalls the earlier description of designers' deliberate interventions aimed at extending and opening the design task. This repeat from an analytical view—coupled with the wide range of design approaches represented by the five architects I interviewed—suggests that the interest in questioning familiar working processes is not limited to a few rebels at the edges of design synthesis. Yet the study drawings brought forward in this discussion show that the direct use of graphics as a means of opening the design process is not widespread. Indeed, graphic content as a design issue has largely been appropriated by what has been called the "deconstruction" movement in design, characterized by the work of Eisenman, Tschumi, and others (Papadakis, Cooke, and Benjamin 1989). This movement has imposed a certain ideological and stylistic program on the issue of graphic content that obscures other theoretical aspects. Criticism has focused on deconstruction as a style of design rather than on such underlying issues as *representation, uncertainty,* and *interpretation.* It may be that, as applications are developed in practice and teaching, graphic content as a design issue will provide a new basis for design; it may also be that graphic content will be incorporated more fully in research and development for computer-aided systems for design, along the lines suggested in the appendix.

REFERENCES

De Franclieu, Françoise. 1981. *The Le Corbusier Sketchbooks,* ed. Françoise De Franclieu, vol. 2. New York: Architectural History Foundation; Cambridge, Mass.: MIT Press.

Eisenman, Peter. 1989. Eisenman builds. *Progressive Architecture* (October): 67-99.

Fish, Stanley. 1980. *Is There a Text in This Class?* Cambridge, Mass.: Harvard College Press.

Le Corbusier. 1960. *My Work.* London: The Architectural Press.

———. 1982. *The Le Corbusier Archive.* Vol. 20, *Ronchamp, Maisons Jaoul, and Other Buildings and Projects.* New York: Garland Publishers; Paris: Foundation Le Corbusier.

Papadakis, A., C. Cooke, and A. Benjamin, ed. 1989. *Deconstruction/Omnibus Volume.* New York: Rizzoli International Publications, Inc.

Pauly, Daniele. 1980. *Ronchamp, Lecture d'une Architecture.* Paris: A.P.P.U.; Ophrys.

———. 1982. The Chapel of Ronchamp as an example of Le Corbusier's creative process. *The Le Corbusier Archive.* Vol. 20, *Ronchamp, Maisons Jaoul, and Other Buildings and Projects,* pp. ix-xix. New York: Garland Publishers; Paris: Foundation Le Corbusier.

Tschumi, Bernard. 1989. Parc de la Villette, Paris. *Deconstruction/Omnibus Volume,* ed. A. Papadakis, C. Cooke, A. Benjamin, pp. 175-81. New York: Rizzoli International Publications, Inc.

White, Edward T. 1986. *Space Adjacency Analysis.* Tucson, Ariz.: Architectural Media Ltd.

Yessios, Chris I. 1987. A fractal studio. *The Proceedings of the 1987 Acadia Workshop,* ed. Barbara-Jo Novitski, pp. 169-81. [United States] Association for Computer-Aided Design in Architecture.

The previous chapter examined graphic processes in design by analyzing study drawings on the page; it proposed an elemental drawing cycle comprising marks and interpretations. The analysis need not stop with external evidence on the drawing page, however: this chapter will continue the examination by an analysis of internal mental processes.

The growing field of cognitive psychology—concerning the act of knowing—offers a way to understand the mental processes involved in making marks and interpreting them. Like the drawing process, the cognitive process in design is cyclic. The interaction of these two processes is the concern of the third epistemological property of study drawings: *study drawings provide a means for cycles of graphic and cognitive processes to interact; their interaction is the source of information generated within the design task.*

THE BASIC COGNITIVE CYCLE: VIEWING A COMPLETED DRAWING

The analysis of drawing and cognition will begin with the simplest case of graphic/cognitive interaction: seeing a completed drawing. I will use Le Corbusier's June 6 charcoal sketch plan of Ronchamp again as a focus for the discussion, and assume that a viewer who is conversant with architectural drawings is seeing the completed drawing (as in figure 4-6) for the first time.

Seeing Le Corbusier's sketch is not one simple act but a complex pattern of activities. The viewer must direct attention toward the drawing, disregard other potential data from the environment, form structures out of the patterns of light and dark contrasts within his or her visual system, identify the drawing as a plan by comparing it with remembered images of other architectural drawings, understand where Le Corbusier intended to put enclosures and openings, respond to the expressive movement of the charcoal lines, feel the emotional potential of the sweeping forms, and combine all of these responses into memory structures associated with terms such as *Le Corbusier, drawing,* or *modern architecture.*

This description names the activities in seeing and gives them an intelligible order. The order is too sequential, however: a first action, a next one, a next. Such a linear description does not explain how emotional responses might influence perception, or how memory contributes to understanding. And the descrip-

5

COMBINED GRAPHIC AND COGNITIVE PROCESSES

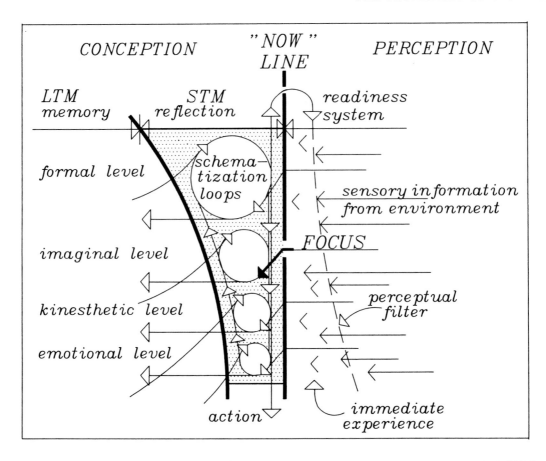

FIGURE 5-1. A functional model of cognitive processes (after Charles Rusch). The model is organized around a NOW line that divides CONCEPTION on the left and PERCEPTION on the right. Conception is made up of short-term memory (STM) and long-term memory (LTM); perception includes immediate experience separated from potential sensory information from the environment by a perceptual filter. Incoming sensory information is reduced through the perceptual filter and recoded into preferred structures of meaning. As new information is received from the environment, immediate action is taken based on this new information, or the information is passed on to be schematized into memory, or both. Development of the diagram adds a series of four interconnected schematization loops based on levels of childhood cognitive development: the emotional, kinesthetic, imaginal, and formal levels. The emotional level concerns basic emotions; the kinesthetic concerns physical movement of the individual's own body; the imaginal includes mental images of the self and the environment; the formal has to do with rational thought, grammatical and logical rules, and mathematical and physical laws. The relative sizes of the loops reflect the amount of schematization required to make structures at each level.

As the arrows show, each loop has three information inputs: from LTM, from other loops, or from immediate experience. From these inputs new symbols are constructed or old ones modified in the loops. Each loop also has four outputs: to LTM as structures for storage, to any other loop for further schematization, to action as triggers for muscular response, or to operate the perceptual filter. This last output acts as a readiness system to anticipate what the system is likely to perceive. In schematization—the construction or modification of symbols—the new information is represented symbolically and woven into the individual's meaning system or memory. *Courtesy Charles Rusch.*

tion does not account for the subjective experience that viewing the drawing is a coherent activity, not separate and sequential but continuous and simultaneous. Yet if the linear order does not serve, what will? Some names and some order are necessary for understanding, not only to deal with the complexities of perception and cognition in seeing a completed drawing, but (later) to consider the further complexities of drawings that are incomplete and in process. The analysis will need an ordering tool or model that is less sequential, that identifies perceptual and cognitive processes less

statically and describes their interactions in nonlinear terms that are applicable to design.

Architect Charles Rusch (1970) has proposed such a model. Based on cognitive studies by such authors as Piaget and Bruner in developmental psychology and Werner and Kaplan in symbol formation, Rusch's model also agrees with Stent's description of abstraction and structuring in chapter 4. The model is directly applicable to the examination of study drawings because it accounts for design as a cyclic, interactive process; it shows how different kinds of experience can be brought into design by images; and it allows an analysis of how marks and interpretation are related. A simplified version of Rusch's model (the diagram in figure 5-1 with its extended caption) sets out the basic terms and ideas about cognition.

With the aid of Rusch's model it will be possible to consider again the cognitive/interpretive processes involved in viewing Le Corbusier's drawing—now in terms more suited to design, and with perception included as an integral part of cognition. Embedding the plan in a diagram of the model (figure 5-2) provides a nonlinear setting for a complex scenario with many feedback channels:

PERCEPTION

Incoming sensory information about the drawing is processed through the perceptual filter, not as through a passive sieve, but through an active sensing layer that anticipates what is to be seen and recodes the information into preferred categories of meaning; this part of the system makes "learned" decisions about what is to be seen based on past experience and on context. Thus, if the Ronchamp plan is in an architectural book or on a drawing board, it will be perceived as a drawing; if it is on a traffic sign, it will be ignored as meaningless vandalism. If context and experience confirm it to be a drawing, the whole figure is located against its ground, the irregular and incomplete lines suggest that it is to be interpreted as a rough freehand sketch rather than a technical diagram. High-contrast areas are given priority as emphatic reference elements for the lighter lines; the lack of a straight baseline or converging lines provides clues that this is not to be read as an elevation or a perspective and is therefore hypothesized to be a floor plan—all prereflective responses performed by the primary receptors of the visual system.

MEMORY AND SCHEMATIZATION

Since this recorded primary information has little emotional or formal content—no flashing lights and sirens, no fine print—most of it enters the reflection part of the system at the imaginal level and—by empathy with the graphic gesture—at the kinesthetic level. No immediate action—like fight or flight—is called for so the information is passed on to the schematization loops. Here the new information is woven into symbolic meaning structures

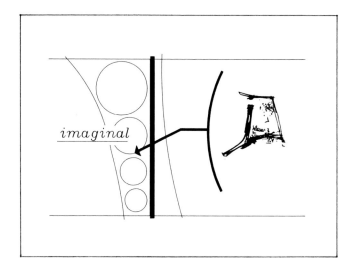

FIGURE 5-2. Cognitive/interpretive processes involved in viewing a completed drawing such as Le Corbusier's charcoal drawing of June 6 for Ronchamp. *Courtesy Daniel Herbert/Le Corbusier, © 1922 ARS, N.Y./SPADEM, Paris.*

by calling up other structures from long-term memory at any of the four levels. The basic cognitive cycle for perceiving the image of Le Corbusier's drawing calls up an array of memories: emotional and kinesthetic memories, say, of having seen the chapel itself; kinesthetic memories of having made charcoal drawings; formal memories of the conventions of floor plans; imaginal and formal memories from having seen other drawings of Ronchamp and having read analyses about them. The new information is interpreted to become congruent with existing cognitive structures, and, in the same operation, the existing structures are continuously interpreted to accept as much of the incoming new information as they can; this weaving together of interpretations confers meaning. The evolving meaning structure of the drawing also builds in an imprint of the immediate circumstances—ambient sound, mood, etc.—and a record of untraceable associations with the designer's whole range of experiences, both personal and professional.

ACTION

Two kinds of action may be required: first, deliberate motor action is needed. If, for example, the viewer is a student working on a formal class assignment that requires tracing a plan for a report on Le Corbusier, then other memories are called up, more schematizations engaged, and appropriate pencil-pushing signals sent to the muscular system. Second, an automatic cognitive action is an essential part of the overall structuring process. This automatic action resets the readiness system to anticipate the next increments of incoming information—say, "the character of this drawing suggests that the next image on the page may be another drawing of Ronchamp."

NEW MENTAL INFORMATION SENT TO MEMORY

The whole elaborate fabric of meanings joins the growing structure of long-term memory; the mental image of the completed Ronchamp drawing, now enriched with new information and complex associations touching other aspects of the individual's life experience, is ready to be called up in a new cognitive cycle and modified by combination with some next experience. Thus design information is not limited in application to some next design task but can be carried into a designer's other concerns.

This is a better description. Its stated feedbacks and its tie to the two-dimensional model temper its naming of specific activities and its sequential order enough to provide a satisfactory idea of the basic cognitive cycle.

The parts and the whole of the cognitive cycle are subject to the mediating effects described in the earlier chapters: pre-existing order, perceptual and cognitive structuring, built-in uncertainty, the culturally imposed grid. Even the simplest case of graphic/cognitive interaction is influenced by these mediating effects. These effects separate the assumed viewer of Le Corbusier's plan from any direct experience of the completed drawing.

This analysis of the basic cognitive cycle brings forward two points. First, viewing the completed drawing generates new information because it makes new cognitive structures: new cognitive structures are new information and new meanings for the individual. Second, interpretation pervades the whole process: to see a completed drawing is to interpret it within a cultural and a personal context. Viewing is always mediated.

Yet, as the discussion has pointed out before, completed drawings do not happen all at once. Designers in the working process of design deal mostly with in-process, incomplete drawings, building them in elemental drawing cycles: mark, interpretation, mark. . . . How does

the cognitive cycle work when it encounters not a completed drawing but an incomplete one—that is, how do cognitive and drawing cycles interact?

THE COGNITIVE CYCLE AND THE DRAWING CYCLE: INCOMPLETE DRAWINGS

To explain how the cognitive/interpretive cycle and the drawing cycle interact, I will continue to use Le Corbusier's charcoal plan for Ronchamp as a subject, focusing now on the south wall. As noted for the examination of the east wall in chapter 4, the point here will not be to discover some supposed "real" starting point and sequence, but to analyze the interactions between the evolving graphic image and the designer's cognitive system.

The following scenario will describe the drawing and cognitive cycles for those marks that make up the south wall—as if watching Le Corbusier add them, one at a time, to his earlier double-like sketch. At each cycle, Le Corbusier perceives and thus interprets the new state of the drawing forwarded from the previous stage, brings up relevant images from memory for reschematization, takes action by making a new mark that alters the whole composition on the page, and prompts a new perception and interpretation in the next cycle. These seamless steps are described in detail only for the first cycle, since subsequent cycles follow the same processes.

PERCEPTION

New information forwarded by the previously made double-line drawing (figure 5-3a, START) includes the figure/ground relationship of the building plan to the whole site, the specific shape of all exterior spaces (especially the entrance space and assembly space, noted earlier by Le Corbusier as critical issues), and the difference between the concave form made by the sharp bend in the south wall and that made by the smooth curve of the east wall.

MEMORY

Structures brought forward from long-term memory include images of previously seen graphic compositions (imaginal/formal levels) and images of previously seen shapes of spaces (all four levels).

SCHEMATIZATION

The schematization loops form meaning structures that are congruent with information from memory and perception; comparison of south and east spaces shows that the wall forming the edge of the south space is not as smooth a curve as the corresponding wall forming the edge of the east space; the abrupt bend in the south wall should be smoothed out (imaginal level).

DELIBERATE ACTION

Starting at the southeast end of the existing line, a new smoothing line is drawn to about half-way along the long leg of the angle, leaving about half of the wall still straight (figure 5-3b).

AUTOMATIC ACTION

The future readiness system is set to compare the shapes of the south and east spaces.

NEW MENTAL INFORMATION

Newly schematized structures are kept in short-term memory: the shape of the south space and the thickness of the south wall.

NEW GRAPHIC INFORMATION FORWARDED TO NEXT CYCLE

The concave forms at the south and east are now more similar; the plan does not show any entrance to the building.

In the next (second) cycle Le Corbusier erases part of the wall to make an entry (figure 5-3c); in the third cycle he notes the jamb at the entry with a short mark (as architects often do to designate openings) and then, for symmetry, puts another at the southeast end of the wall (figure 5-3d); in the fourth cycle he adds another curve to fill in the thin, straight part of the wall (figure 5-3e).

Something unexpected happens at the end of the fourth step in the scenario, however. The new graphic

5-3a. START.

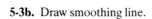

5-3b. Draw smoothing line.

5-3c. Erase to make entry.

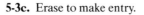

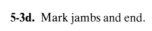

5-3d. Mark jambs and end.

5-3e. Draw filling line.

FIGURE 5-3a through e. Cognitive/interpretive processes involved in viewing and working on an incomplete drawing: a hypothetical scenario for Le Corbusier's development of the south wall in his charcoal drawing of June 6 for Ronchamp. *© 1922 ARS, N.Y./SPADEM, Paris.*

information available for interpretation in a next (fifth) cycle includes more than just the charcoal mark made in the fourth. A new design issue has emerged: the thickness of the south wall. According to this scenario, the thickness of the south wall was neither preconceived as a mental image nor preselected as a subject for study, but found as an artifact of the graphic working process. The increments of new information produced within each cycle—undertaken to refine certain limited objectives—may, when taken together, present a potential reorganization of a major part of the composition. Suddenly it appears that the south wall might be more than a separation between inside and outside with a certain bend to it—it might become a volume in itself.

INCREMENTAL REFINEMENTS AND MAJOR REORGANIZATIONS

The scenario for the south wall illustrates two kinds of newly generated graphic information: incremental refinements and a major reorganization.[1] The following discussion will consider each of these in turn.

Incremental refinements, shown in the scenario's first four cycles, produce new information by considering a graphic element (or a group of them) in the drawing and adjusting it to improve its fit, however the designer might define it, within the design task. Information is created as the designer makes some graphic mark "A," and then interprets that mark as "more than A." Or, less formally, one might say that designers read more information out of the drawing than they have put into it. This almost routine step-by-step production is possible because, as this discussion holds, each mark becomes a new element immediately upon notation— not just on the page but in the conceptual scope of the design task. Not only does each mark acquire a graphic context at the instant it is made, but it alters the context of all the preceding marks; and, especially in study drawings, the meaning of any mark depends absolutely

on its context.[2] Thus each mark made in pursuit of incremental refinements demands a reinterpretation of the whole graphic context even as it itself constitutes a new subject for interpretation.

Not all incremental refinements succeed in moving the development along. Some lead to dead ends—whatever efforts went toward developing the crescent-shaped esplanade for the Ronchamp outside assembly area, for example—though they do produce information at the moment. Other incremental refinements may generate negative information; that is, information about what ought not to be done. For example, one of Le Corbusier's two follow-up pencil studies on June 6, 1950, relocates the main entrance of the chapel toward the altar end of the building, an absurd idea that involves a tortuous entrance path and crowds the front part of interior space (figure 5-4). The notion of negative information recalls Esherick's comment about arbitrarily changing something in the drawing just to see what the consequences are: both Le Corbusier and Esherick know that drawing may be used experimentally. They understand that, as in other fields, graphic experiments may produce failures as well as successes, or possibly interesting unexpected effects. Dead ends, negative results, and happy accidents all produce information in just the same way as do the directly productive incremental refinements: they demand reinterpretation.

Even larger reinterpretations are demanded by major reorganizations because they bring new issues into the design task. Examples from Ronchamp illustrate the varieties of major reorganizations and their operation in generating information. Given Pauly's "four-line" premise as a beginning and the built project as an end, there appear to be three major reorganizations for the Ronchamp plan: the volume of the south wall, as a "found" issue; the addition of the three chapels, introduced as a chosen issue in the first pencil follow-up study on June 6 (figure 4-3); and the change from the proposed full development of the east esplanade to the reduced development actually built, an issue that may have been forced by budget pressure (figure 4-2). These three types of reorganization—*found, chosen,*

[1]The terms *incremental refinement* and *major reorganization* are taken from Rusch (1969). Ullman, in his analysis of the mechanical engineering design process (Ullman, Wood, and Craig 1990), recognizes only a kind of incremental refinement and does not discuss major reorganizations.

[2]A graphic mark like a symbol of a doorswing in architectural working drawings might be said to have a meaning even when taken out of its specific context; but, in study drawings, doorswing symbols, even if shown, are incidental unless the subject has to do specifically with the arc of a swinging door.

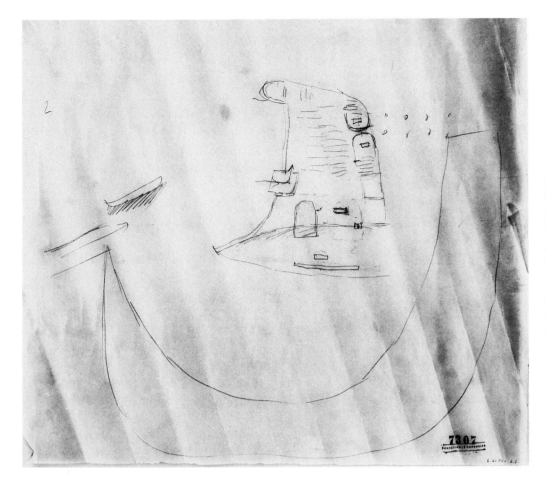

FIGURE 5-4. Le Corbusier: study sketch plan for the chapel at Ronchamp, June 6, 1950. Pencil on heavy tracing paper; same 1:200 scale as the charcoal drawing. At 640mm × 560mm, this drawing page is almost exactly the same size as the drawing shown in figure 4-3 and is executed in the same media. Presumably this is a second overlay on the charcoal drawing of June 6. In addition to varying the entrance location, Le Corbusier changed the location of both the interior and the exterior pulpit and altar. © *1922 ARS, N.Y./ SPADEM, Paris.*

and *forced*—might apply to any project, from a church to a chair. Only the first two, because they are graphically originated reorganizations, require further discussion here.

By definition, found reorganizations occur as a potential result of a series of incremental refinements whose graphic image suggests some new direction. These reorganizations do not happen automatically as a routine product of the working process the way incremental refinements do. Instead, the designer must recognize the opportunity presented on the page, must reinterpret a whole bloc of the graphic context, must stop directing incremental refinements toward one objective and start directing them toward another. As Rusch (1969) points out, such reorganizations may involve the whole project, a major or minor part, or some still more subordinate part. In the reorganization of the south wall of Ronchamp, for example, Le Corbusier had to recognize that this discovered thickness was a new design issue in its own right, a candidate for a new sequence of incremental refinements. With hindsight

granted by the completed building, it is possible to see that this reorganization opened the way eventually to develop the dramatic volume of the completed wall.[3] Of course, Le Corbusier, like any architect in the midst of the working process, could not know exactly where a reorganization would end—as the fate of the east esplanade proves.

Chosen reorganization is also a graphic artifact in that it is likely to occur only if a designer becomes dissatisfied with the outcome of graphic incremental refinements and chooses a new direction. Finding the roots of new directions in design is outside the graphic focus of this discussion, except to note that graphic exploration must be an essential precondition for reor-

---

[3]It is true that Le Corbusier did not pursue the issue of the thick south wall right away. In the two other drawings from the same day (figures 4-3 and 5-4) the south wall turns into one line, and chapter 4 notes that the south wall did not take on its full thickness until more than two years later. Nevertheless, it is clear that the thickness of the south wall originated from the buildup of incremental refinements made in the June 6 charcoal drawing.

ganization; that is, reorganization implies some previous organization, which must have been expressed graphically. Unsatisfactory graphic refinements show that a new direction is necessary. A related action by choice is the importation of some new bloc of information into the design task, such as Le Corbusier's using a crab shell as a conceptual model for the roof of Ronchamp.[4] Other objects, other drawings, or other life experiences also can serve as massive infusions of new information. Until they are incorporated into the graphic context of the design task, however, they have only the limited capacity of generating information attributed above to completed drawings.

Reorganization by choice surfaced in the interviews with both Esherick and Jahn. Esherick became dissatisfied with incremental refinements in one of his drawings for a residential project:

> It seemed to me that this wasn't the sort of thing that she [the client] would want, that this was standing out, that this tower expressing the circular stair was basically not a good idea.... Then I had to figure out how to get the stair someplace else, so the next thing was this idea of coming in here and ... the spiral stair would be here and you go around it....

Jahn described a major reorganization of the whole scheme after the first stage of the competition for the American Airlines terminal at the John F. Kennedy Airport:

> It was a competition where we didn't have any reaction, we just had to do something, and the competition took longer to decide and I made actually some of the [revised] sketches while I was flying around in the world ... and there was something that bugged me, and I made those sketches and the client called us and said, "You won the competition but there's a couple things we don't like," and I said, "Well, what [are they]?, and ... frankly, I've got another idea."

---

[4]Le Corbusier (1957, 89-90): "The shell of a crab picked up on Long Island near New York in 1946 is lying on my drawing board. It will become the roof of the chapel: two membranes of concrete six centimeters thick and 2m.26cm. apart. The shell will lie on walls made of the salvaged stones."

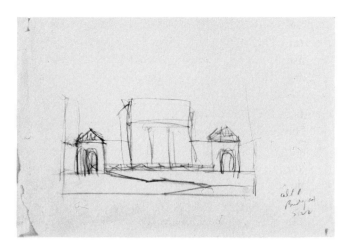

FIGURE 5-5. Robert Stern: study drawings for U.S. Embassy annex, Budapest, Hungary, May 22, 1989. Soft pencil on lightweight tracing paper; approximately 16″ × 11″. The pencil note reads "Alt 1 / 5 22." At the same height, with the same media, and concerned with the same issues, this drawing is presumably from the same drawing sequence as that of figure 1-9. *Courtesy Robert A.M. Stern Architects.*

Stern described a related example—perhaps a combination of negative experiment and chosen reorganization—concerning his work on the U.S. Embassy annex in Budapest. As the text of the interview shows, Stern considered the street facade to be a critical issue for this project. He had developed a promising direction based on modifications of the composite photocopy from Lutyens's work (figure 4-13), but found that the given program did not require enough space to fill the volume implied by the facade.

> This ... drawing is a totally wild-card idea in the sense that if we had such a small program and we had to be a high building, what would happen if we made a low base along the side and tied these two small functions into a kind of tower in the middle? A really horrible idea in my opinion, but one that had to be studied. (figure 5-5)

Here, Stern was dissatisfied with the prospects for reconciling his original graphic image of the facade with the program. He tried a reorganization, not to see if it would work, but rather to confirm—graphically—that it would not.

In contrast to the examples from Esherick, Jahn, and Stern, Eisenman's process seems to preclude major reorganizations, either found or chosen. He has effectively defined a satisfactory solution as the graphic and then spatial documentation of whatever happens when a certain drawing strategy is applied to a certain design premise. Even here, however, a designer's presence is required: first to select the premise and the strategy, then to set them going, and finally to interpret the results of their collision.

These contemporary examples, following the discussion of the development of the south wall and the reorganizations of Ronchamp, show that both types of graphic development—incremental refinement and major reorganization—produce information by continuous reinterpretations of the graphic context as it evolves. These reinterpretations of the graphic context are accomplished through interactions between the always incomplete study drawing and the designer's cognitive system. The same basic cognitive processes take place in reading incomplete drawings as in reading complete ones, but the interaction between the cognitive system and the incomplete drawings is more complex. This more complex interaction produces the added measure of information that moves the design task forward.

TWO KEY GRAPHIC/COGNITIVE INTERACTIONS

From the discussion of the graphic/cognitive interaction above it is possible to specify the two key interactions that provide the means for generating information in the design task.

DRAWING

As a deliberate action, the designer introduces a new element into his or her own perceptual field (figure 5-6). Typically this new element is a graphic mark made on the study drawing page, but it also may be the current study drawing read in some new way—a found reorganization. Or, the new element may be some completed drawing or other element, provided that it has been incorporated into the study drawings to become a part of the graphic dialogue of the design task (Le Corbusier must *draw* the crab-shell-as-roof, for example, not just think about it). Furthermore, the designer must have a specific, but not necessarily consciously stated, intention toward the new element: namely, that it is to be interpreted.

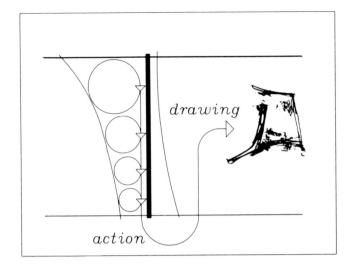

FIGURE 5-6. The designer's action of drawing introduces a new element into the perceptual field. © *1922 ARS, N.Y./SPADEM, Paris.*

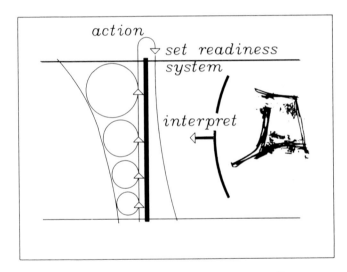

FIGURE 5-7. The designer's action of setting the readiness system prepares to interpret the drawing. © *1922 ARS, N.Y./SPADEM, Paris.*

INTERPRETING

As a tacit (or, in the term used in the scenarios above, automatic) action, the designer sets the readiness part of the cognitive system (figure 5-7) to regard the study drawing page, including the new element, as mutable, and so to regard the marks themselves as ambiguous—that is, as subject to more than one interpretation. The readiness system actively anticipates the nature of incoming information; it includes not only the immediate perceptual filter, but long-range expectations about what the individual will encounter in the perceptual field. The designer has had to learn through education and practice how to set the readiness system to function within the design task, to regard study drawings as ambiguous. The ambiguity of study drawings deserves its own discussion, which I will pursue in chapter 7; here I will note only that this possibility of multiple interpretations of study drawings is what permits the designer to read more out of a mark or a drawing than went into it: to generate information. The designer has also had to learn to express the enriched interpretation as a deliberate action; that is, to project a new element into his or her own perceptual field—starting a new cycle by drawing.

Although these two key interactions are discussed here as separate entities in separate operations, the designer's drawing and interpretation are not themselves separate, but continuous and simultaneous. They form a condensed, tightly cycled internal dialogue between the designer as drawer and the designer as interpreter, creating information through new meanings assigned to drawings that are taken to be ambiguous. This gain of information is not unrestricted, however; although the dialogue is open both to new meanings and to the inherent uncertainty of the process, it is still subject to the limitations of the designer's experience and the effects of the culturally determined grid discussed in earlier chapters. The earlier discussion of these two restrictions—uncertainty and the grid—can be carried further now by using the two key graphic/cognitive interactions as a reference.

UNCERTAINTY RECONSIDERED

Chapter 4 described how some designers deliberately look for geometric constraints or other discrepant devices to overcome the limitations of their individual experience in design: to introduce uncertainty. Now, having examined *drawing* and *interpreting* in more detail, it is possible to extend the earlier analysis and find a new basis for understanding uncertainty. Peter Eisenman's Cincinnati DAAP project (figure 4-10) will again provide a subject for the analysis.

Eisenman's parti sketches, including their radial line constraints, look like any other collection of incremental refinements associated with forms and spaces. All the marks in the parti have been drawn as a deliberate act, apparently in just the terms used above to describe the *drawing* action; but in the *interpreting* action, the marks referring to geometric constraints resist being treated like the marks of the parti that refer to forms and spaces. The special marks that signify geometric constraints are given a distinctive interpretation.

This distinctive interpretation entails the designer's taking the special marks of the constraint as unambiguous: their meaning is fixed. Their fixed, unambiguous meaning is that the designer must consult the rules that have been associated with the constraint. As chapter 4 noted for the Wexner Center, such fixed marks and their associated rules produce uncertainty directly because of unforeseen collisions and the cascade of secondary effects. Now, with a clearer sense of interpretation's role in the working process, another, indirect aspect of this deliberate uncertainty becomes apparent: the designer must interpret not only the foreground design issues and the effects of unforeseen collisions, but also the rules of the geometric constraint. Rules as well as marks get involved in the designer's reschematization of the design task, introducing still another sort of uncertainty.

The intrusion of fixed meanings and the interpretation of rules bring the specialized marks of the geometric constraint into a peculiar position: they exist somewhere between the background and the foreground of the design task. These marks are not quite background design statements because the designer must acknowledge them; they are not quite foreground statements because their graphic meaning is fixed and the designer's treatment of them is displaced to interpreting the rules associated with them. In Eisenman's work, this position between background and foreground is compounded with other "between" and "displaced" positions, since his stated intent is to locate architectural meaning between such imposed polarities as form and function, past and present (Eisenman 1989, 151). Thus Eisenman's geometric constraints are part of a larger program to locate architecture outside traditional meaning systems.

This extended analysis of deliberate uncertainty could equally well have treated the formal anomaly of Esherick's factory window or the adopted image of Stern's photocopy. Both show the designer's deliberate introduction of devices to shock the working process and so extend the design task outside the limitations of his own current experience. Thus the deliberate device represents uncertainty—what cannot be known by the designer from within the design task.

UNCERTAINTY AND THE GRID

What cannot be known from within the design task has come up before in this discussion: the culturally imposed grid described in chapter 3. There the discussion noted that the grid normally seems transparent and neutral; its effects in determining the "natural" way of acquiring knowledge are a part of the tacit background, unformulated and hence unaccessible. Like the deliberate device to introduce uncertainty, the grid imposes its structure on all the foreground activities of the design task. Unlike the deliberate device, however, the grid is out of the designer's control. The designer can control the deliberate device, can specify what it is and how it is to work, but he or she cannot control the unformulated background that is the grid.

Yet there is a sort of forced relation between the deliberate device and the grid. Imposing a deliberate, controlled device—such as a geometric constraint, a formal anomaly, or an adopted image—on the design task allows the designer access to gridlike information. Such information is not a concealed part of some "real" grid, but a substitute for it that produces analogous effects. The deliberate device becomes a surrogate for the grid: it acknowledges the artifice of the tacit background and the consequent artifice of design by introducing an expressed issue—almost in the foreground of the design task—that the designer can and must confront. Imposing a deliberate and arbitrary device acts as if a

part of the grid's invisible grain were visible, as if a part of its forced intention were voluntary, and as if part of its hidden loss of information were exposed. Thus, besides representing uncertainty, the deliberate device also represents the unknowable impositions of the designer's parent culture in the design task.

Although both drawing and interpretation occur as part of making study drawings for a particular design task, they involve more than just manipulating visual images and they go beyond the designer's professional training and practice. Making study drawings not only moves the design task forward by involving the designer's whole experience, but it adds to that experience. Design drawing is not just a series of tricks for handling visual images to solve puzzles, it is a way of understanding.

REFERENCES

Eisenman, Peter. 1989. Blue line text. *Deconstruction/ Omnibus Volume,* ed. A. Papadakis, C. Cooke, A. Benjamin, pp. 150-51. New York: Rizzoli International Publications, Inc.

Le Corbusier. 1957. *The Chapel at Ronchamp.* New York: Frederick A. Praeger.

Rusch, Charles W. 1969. On the use of leveling and sharpening as an analytic tool in the study of artistic behavior. *Proceedings, 77th Annual Convention.* American Psychological Association. Pp. 478-79.

———. 1970. Understanding awareness. *Journal of Aesthetic Education* October 4 (4): 57-79.

Ullman, David G., Stephen Wood, and David Craig. 1990. The importance of drawing in the mechanical design process. *Computers and Graphics* 14 (2).

When architectural designers collaborate on a project, they get together in frequent short meetings to coordinate their work. At these meetings, a tacit structure of graphic conventions frames the talk as well as the drawings: "this axis [*of the plan*]," or "that pattern of openings [*on the elevation*]." Such working meetings may last just a few minutes or tens of minutes—only long enough to set a direction for the next session of solitary work that is also, inescapably, conceived in terms of graphic conventions. Thus graphic conventions pervade the work through two complementary functions, providing not only a conceptual framework for an individual to make the drawings but also a common ground for a collective audience to consider them.

These two functions of graphic conventions in the working process may be stated more exactly as the fourth property of study drawings: *study drawings embody graphic conventions as a basis for ordering cognitive images and for enabling communication in the working process of design.*

To consider both these functions, I will examine first the relation of graphic conventions to cognitive processes—implicitly the cognitive processes of an individual working alone. And second, as I survey the role of graphic conventions in communication, I will include accounts of working groups in the firms I visited.

6

GRAPHIC CONVENTIONS

ORDERING COGNITIVE IMAGES

Those trained to grasp a drawing at a glance can find their desired information immediately.

CHARLES G. RAMSEY and HAROLD R. SLEEPER, in the preface to the first edition of *Architectural Graphic Standards*

Grasping a drawing at a glance requires the reader's cognitive readiness system to expect certain kinds of information—not just about the drawing's content, but about the form the drawing will take. Users of *Architectural Graphic Standards* know that all its drawings have a ready-made form based on a set of familiar graphic conventions. Every drawing in the book—except conceptual constructions such as graphs and tables (which have their own conventions)—is either a plan, elevation, section, perspective, or axonometric drawing derived from Euclidean geometry (figure 6-1). It is these five

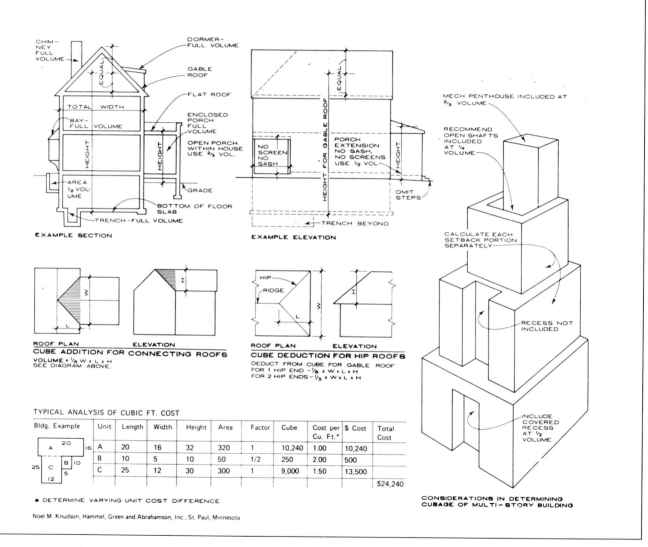

ARCHITECTURAL VOLUME OF BUILDINGS

The ARCHITECTURAL VOLUME (cube or cubage) of a building is the sum of the products of the areas defined on previous page (using the area of a single story for multistory portions having the same area on each floor) and the height from the underside of the lowest floor construction system to the average height of the surface of the finished roof above for the various parts of the building.

From AIA Document D101, 1967

CUBAGE includes the following volumes, taken in full:

The cubic content of the actual space enclosed within the outer surfaces of the exterior or outer walls and contained between the outside of the roof and the bottom of the lowest floor; bays, oriels, dormers, penthouses; chimneys; walk through tunnels; tanks, vaults, pits and trenches, if made of building construction materials (not simple earth excavations); enclosed porches and balconies, including screened areas.

The CUBAGE includes the following volumes in part:

a) Two-thirds ($^2/_3$) volume for:
Non-enclosed porches, if recessed into the building and not having enclosing sash or screens.

b) One-half ($^1/_2$) volume for:
Non-enclosed porches built as an extension to the building, without enclosing sash or screens.

Areaways and pipe tunnels.

Patio areas that have building walls extended on two sides, roof over and paved surfacing.

The CUBAGE does not include the following features:

The cubage of outside steps, terraces, courts, garden walls; light shafts, parapets, cornices, roof overhangs; footings, deep foundations, piling, caissons, special foundations and similar features. Note: In making cubic foot cost analysis, as a matter of information and reference, it is recommended that cost items such as piling, caissons, deep foundations, unusual step construction and other non-typical features be listed as factors having an effect on the unit cost without being included in the cubage.

CUBIC FOOT COST

The CUBIC FOOT COST equals the net cost divided by the total cubage.

The NET COST in usual practice includes the following:

The building construction, including built-in cabinets and furniture, all finishes and hardware; mechanical work, including plumbing, heating, air conditioning and controls; electrical work, lighting fixtures, sound and signal systems; elevators; sprinklers; equipment provided for the operation of the building.

The NET COST usually excludes the following:

Furniture and furnishings, such as ranges, laundry and kitchen equipment, clocks, lockers, files; organs; draperies, shades, blinds, awnings; non-built in furniture; roads, walks, terraces, and other site development; landscaping; sewage disposal system; power plant; wells or other water supply; utilities to the building. Also fees for Architects, Engineers and specialty consultants.

TYPICAL ANALYSIS OF CUBIC FT. COST

Bldg. Example	Unit	Length	Width	Height	Area	Factor	Cube	Cost per Cu. Ft.*	$ Cost	Total Cost
	A	20	16	32	320	1	10,240	1.00	10,240	
	B	10	5	10	50	1/2	250	2.00	500	
	C	25	12	30	300	1	9,000	1.50	13,500	
										$24,240

♣ DETERMINE VARYING UNIT COST DIFFERENCE

Noel M. Knudson; Hammel, Green and Abrahamson, Inc.; St. Paul, Minnesota

FIGURE 6-1. Typical page from *Architectural Graphic Standards* (sixth edition). Axonometric drawing is not shown. *From Architectural Graphic Standards, sixth edition; editor: Joseph N. Boaz, AIA; copyright © 1970 by John Wiley & Sons, Inc. Reprinted by permission of John Wiley & Sons, Inc. Original drawing by Noel M. Knudsen; Hammell, Green and Abrahamson, Inc., St. Paul, Minnesota.*

graphic conventions[1] that permit the quick access to information implied by such terms as *grasp* and *glance* in the epigraph above.

Even quick access is mediated, however: the supposed immediate access is less direct than it seems. The discussion in chapter 4 established that graphic form is neither neutral nor transparent, so graphic conventions necessarily affect the nature of the information presented in the drawing. These effects are not restricted to finely finished drawings such as those in *Architectural Graphic Standards*. The same effects are also found in study drawings, which use the same conventions.

The plan, elevation, section, perspective, and axonometric conventions used in study drawings provide readymade structures that classify—or, rather, become—the substance of the design task. Even nonconventional experience must become conventionalized if it is to be included in the work: although introspection suggests that architects can experience and remember forms and spaces without using architectural graphic conventions, any recording, analysis, or application of these experiences in design is always channelled into certain forms of graphic conventions.[2] This channelling is no coincidence. Graphic functions within the design task are structured and classified according to these particular conventions because architectural education and practice are conducted largely through their use. Each use predisposes every next use, so that these conventions come to pervade the design task and thereby influence not just what architects *do* think, but what architects *can* think.

I asked Peter Eisenman about the influence of graphic conventions on architectural thinking:

DH: Architects learn certain conventions for drawing; do you think these conventions affect the way they experience space?

PE: Sure, no question, it's like toilet training affects how you live your daily life. Any kind of experiential knowledge affects the conceptual framework or apparatus. I mean, I absolutely think that we see . . . [pause]. I believe an architectural historian should be trained as an architect, or an architectural critic should be trained as an architect, because they can't see otherwise and they don't know how to see the way that architects see. That is, they can't see the way we conceptualize; therefore they can't criticize from inside, and I think it's much better to understand from inside even if you're criticizing from outside.

For Eisenman, conventions affect how architects see because they become part of a general conceptual framework. Yet this is not to say that architects can only experience space as plan, section, etc. Conventions can be necessary without being sufficient or comprehensive. The whole life experience of an architect is not formulated predominantly in terms of training in the use either of plumbing fixtures or of graphic conventions.

The design task is formulated that way, however—predominantly or even exclusively in terms of graphic conventions.[3] As noted in chapter 4, most designers assume that the graphic conventions learned through education and practice will enable them to represent directly whatever is important to the content of the design task, although some designers employ deliberate devices to introduce uncertainty. These efforts to introduce uncertainty do not bypass graphic conventions, however, because they and their products are all eventually represented through one of the five graphic conventions. Graphic conventions even decide what kinds of information will count as knowledge; they influence what seems "natural" to include in the work.

It takes extraordinary effort even to vary these conventions. Such a variation as Eisenman's "axonometric model" from his work on *House X* (figure 6-2) is not a new convention, although it is a valuable demonstration that conventions are arbitrary projections from certain points of view. And Eisenman's "Boolean cube," used to generate the architectural forms for the Carnegie-

---

[1]The term *conventions* is used in various senses—sometimes to mean the five kinds of graphic projections listed here, sometimes more broadly to mean standardized ways of showing dimensions, notations, signs, or symbols. *Plans* are, of course, only horizontal *sections;* I have kept to common usage, which distinguishes between them. I have also kept to common usage in using *axonometric* rather than its subdivisions of *isometric, dimetric,* etc.

---

[2]One could make the case that no experience is nonconventional, but in this discussion I will use the term *nonconventional* to mean *not in the form of any of the five architectural conventions.*

---

[3]The most obvious exception to formulating the design task through graphic conventions is the use of models.

FIGURE 6-2. Peter Eisenman: axonometric model for *House X*. In his book on the house (p. 210), Eisenman says of this model that "the axonometric model . . . changes depending on the position of viewing. From the side and from eye level [left] it is seen as raking in different directions. But from a slightly raised angle on the oblique it is seen as a conventional orthogonal model. Finally, when it is viewed from the oblique at a 45-degree angle with one eye closed [right], it appears to flatten out and assumes the precise aspect of an axonometric drawing." *Courtesy Peter Eisenman.*

Mellon Research Institute and the Pittsburgh Technology Center Building, eventually gets transformed into the conventional Euclidean geometry of plans and elevations.[4]

An application of a truly non-Euclidean convention might be the use of fractal geometry. A recent article on fractals made a reverse connection to design:

> Once one has a command of the fractal language, one can describe the shape of a cloud as precisely and simply as an architect might describe a house with blueprints that use the language of traditional geometry. (Jurgens, Peitgen, and Saupe 1990, 61)

For the discussion of study drawings, this fractal statement might be turned around. One could ask whether special graphic conventions would be required to "de-

scribe a house with blueprints that use the language of fractal geometry." Or one could invert the question to ask what kind of house might result from being described with "blueprints that use the language of fractal geometry, incorporating a set of fractal conventions." An essential consideration in establishing any special conventions (implied by the mention of "blueprints") would be their potential use for construction. It would seem pointless, even if possible, to redescribe a fractal-based design in terms of Euclidean-based conventions in order to communicate the designer's intention to a building industry that only understands plans, elevations, sections, perspectives, and axonometric drawings. Even these first questions about the relationship of alternative graphic conventions to existing ones suggest that design as we know it may be limited to conceiving and building only those things allowed by a given set of Euclidean conventions.

Within a design task that may have unsuspected limitations, then, these five conventions provide a ready-made, economical means for the designer's cognitive

---

[4]See Eisenman, Peter. 1989. Eisenman builds. *Progressive Architecture* (October): 93.

system to generate or perceive images, to store them, and to recall them when needed.

GENERATING AND PERCEIVING IMAGES

In generating and perceiving visual images, graphic conventions provide the connections within the graphic/cognitive cycle discussed in chapters 4 and 5. Both parts of the cycle—that is, both drawing and interpretation—assume a conventional structure: what is drawn is intended to be a plan or a section, for example, and the drawing is similarly perceived and interpreted as a plan or a section.[5] Conventions allow economical cognitive schematization to begin by assuming one of a few possible armatures around which to organize the incoming visual stimuli.

Since study drawings are often so roughly made, conventions are interpreted more freely there than for presentation or working drawings. Indeed, such freedom is part of the ambiguity that is essential for design development. A striking example of free interpretation is the possible cross-conventional reading of plan and section drawings apparent in Le Corbusier's June 6 charcoal sketch. This drawing, intended as a plan, could have been read, even unconsciously, as a section (figure 6-3). Such a cross-conventional reading could have triggered not only a new interpretation of the west wall as a shell form for the roof, but also a related reading of the tapering south wall in plan as a vertical section through the thick and sloping south wall, and a similar free reading of the entrance in plan could suggest the gap between the wall and the roof seen in section.

The freedom of the study drawing format also permits drawings that do not embody one of the five plans, elevation, section, perspective, or axonometric conventions. Such drawings are similar to the graphs and tables noted above in the discussion of *Architectural Graphic Standards*. Conventions are not absent—these drawings merely embody some other conventions. They may use either established conventions such as those of graphs and tables (figure 1-6), the Venn diagrams of

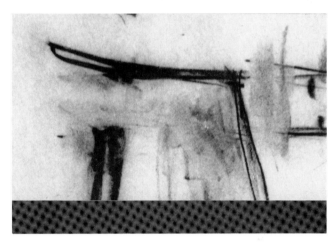

FIGURE 6-3. Le Corbusier: fragment of Ronchamp plan drawing (above) compared with later cross-section looking west (below). The section is one of the series of sections shown on the larger drawing in figure 1-10. (Upper), (lower), *Le Corbusier, © 1922 ARS, N.Y./SPADEM, Paris.*

philosophy (figure 6-4), or special conventions such as those that one person may set up and define on the spot (figure 1-1) or that a small group may agree to observe on a particular occasion.

STORING AND RECALLING IMAGES

In storing and recalling images, graphic conventions provide the means for the cognitive system to bring previous experiences into the design task. My interview with Stanley Tigerman provides a good example of this use of conventions. I questioned him about his reference to a monastic cloister in a study drawing for a house (figure 6-5):

---

[5]Future research will no doubt make further distinctions among conventions: Umberto Eco (1980, 36) notes that "... there are in a design, for example, various systems of notation ... the codes operative in a plan are not quite the same as those operative in a section or in a wiring diagram...."

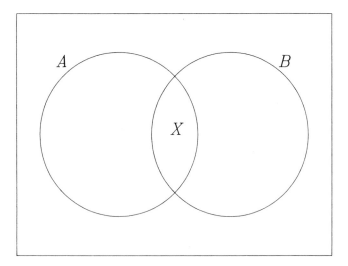

FIGURE 6-4. Venn diagram showing basic logical connections. Such diagrams must be accompanied by a text that defines the terms, such as "A and B are classes; the subclass common to A and B is indicated by X." *Courtesy Daniel Herbert.*

ST: There were two different things, you get this and then you get something in the middle, and here they're expressed as plan types and sectional role types, so the monastic cloister is one that presents another plan type. . . .

DH: This drawing of the cloister, then, is an analytic drawing.

ST: They're analysis, analytic drawings.

DH: But you know about these things; why do you need to draw them here and now on this page?

ST: I think to embed it in my mind.

DH: Is it already embedded?

ST: It must have been because I drew it. I just had to make it clear to me that it counted, that my memory had those things, actually held water for this project.

DH: It appears that your redrawing these analytic drawings is a way of hooking those images up from deeply embedded memory, making them current, so you can use them this time, now.

ST: I think that's probably true.

Tigerman's drawing and his comments about it raise two issues related to storing and recalling images: the cloister drawing's conventionality, and the use of types.

The source of the drawing's conventionality could be Tigerman's own experience in visiting several medieval cloisters. His perceptions could be stored as whole spatial experiences—no doubt structured in some way, but not necessarily according to architectural graphic conventions—and then recalled and reformulated as conventionalized plan and section drawings for current use on the drawing page. That is, conventionalized information within the design task may be a translation from a supposedly nonconventional experience into an explicitly conventional form. A designer might similarly recall the interior space of any building by making a diagrammatic plan or section of it. Tigerman's practice in travel sketches suggests that he often recodes his experience into architectural graphic conventions on the spot. At the time of visiting some cloistered building he would likely have made plan, elevation, section, and perspective drawings. Such drawings would provide a way of storing aspects of the experience into conventionalized images for later recall, perhaps with other images obtained from published references. He could then have brought any one of these already conventionalized images onto the page for current use.

Furthermore, Tigerman refers not just to plans or sections; he labels these parts of the drawing as *plan types* and *sectional role types.* Evidently, he has stored in his long-term memory several conventionalized images of cloisters and, at some time, has abstracted them into types. This additional abstraction suggests that conventions are not just the means for retrieving visual images but can themselves become the subject for further generalized structuring—whatever a designer finds congruent among several cloister plans becomes a cloister plan type.

Robert Stern also discussed the effect of conventions as he described his work on the U.S. Embassy annex in Budapest:

DH: The drawings I've seen here all seem to be according to the conventions we learned in school; all plan, section, elevation, etc. Are there any drawings that embody other, private conventions that only you could interpret?

RS: No, not that I can think of. I don't use axonometric because you don't see buildings in axonometric. I was told, by the way, when I was in school that you don't see buildings in elevation; I don't think that's true, that's a

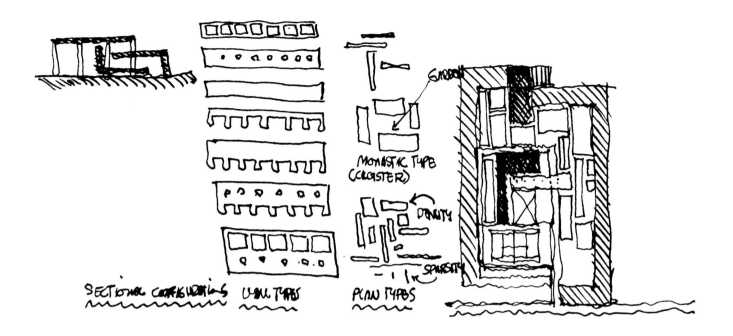

FIGURE 6-5. Stanley Tigerman: sketch for house, Palm Beach, Florida, 1986. Ink on sketchbook page; 8″ × 5″. Number III in a sequence of eight consecutive pages in the sketchbook; see also figure 2-7. The monastic cloister is about in the middle of the drawing, labeled "MONASTIC TYPE / (CLOISTER)." *Courtesy Tigerman McCurry Architects.*

modernist prejudice, but plans, sections, elevations, perspectives are still . . . [trails off].

DH: Do you think that these conventions affect the product of the building?

RS: Your bet, and that's why I try to use as many different ways of studying the project as possible, including modeling to study the mass outside and the spaces inside; we turn out huge models of important rooms and you can put your head in them. . . .

DH: So you never keep working exclusively on, say, a plan for a long time?

RS: No, I would be a very bad architect if I did. And I never study just elevations.

Stern's strategy to avoid becoming trapped by graphic conventions is to bypass them by using large models; he recognizes the pervasive effect of graphic conventions as a condition of design.

It appears from the analysis and the examples thus far that any graphic notations in study drawings, no matter how abstract, are structured according to a few conventions. If the drawings refer directly to some physical aspect of a building, even if they appear to be random scratchings, they will embody one of the five plan, elevation, section, perspective, or axonometric conventions; or, less frequently, they may embody another set of accepted or made-up conventions. These conventions not only provide a ready-made, economical means for the designer's cognitive generation, perception, storage, and recall of images, but also provide for further structuring as a basis for making subsequent abstractions into types.

LIMITATIONS IMPOSED BY CONVENTIONS

As a cost for their cognitive economy, graphic conventions impose the same kind of structuring or formulation limitations that have appeared throughout this discussion; conventions impose structure, and so not only do they cause a loss of information but they constrain what the designer can think about within the design task. I also questioned Peter Eisenman about the limitations of conventions:

> **DH:** Do conventions limit what you can do?
>
> **PE:** Yes, that's why I want to move out of them into computers, because they're not restricted by the same conventions that I am.
>
> **DH:** Do you ask the computer to go beyond these conventions?
>
> **PE:** I don't know enough about computers to know whether I ask it to or not; I've got a little PC myself, but I can't program it. But I'm always trying to break down the conventions, because the conventions repress the capacity to discover.
>
> **DH:** We are taught to believe that we have access to the real world through these conventions. I think we need to be aware of that and at least . . . consent to using them.
>
> **PE:** I would agree to that.

Eisenman's aggressive approach—"trying to break down the conventions"—is consistent with his other efforts to bring the design process out of the tacit background and address it as a foreground issue. Here it appears that he views the computer not as a friendly office helper that will make things go more smoothly, but as a tool for disrupting conventional processes.[6]

Like the other structures that this discussion has described within the design task—pre-existing order, graphic idiom, cognitive schematization—architectural graphic conventions are cultural artifacts that are part of the ordering necessary to get on with the work. And like all such ordering, conventions impose limitations. They exact a cost of lost information, reduced opportunities, and narrowed choices, whether the designer works alone or with others.

How do the same conventions that enable designers to work alone also enable them to work together? Or, more generally, how do graphic conventions enable a designer's study drawings to change from a private to a semi-private audience?

COMMUNICATION IN THE WORKING PROCESS

The definition of a good study drawing from a point of view of its utility in the office is that can I convey what I have in mind to someone else who will have to draw it up, develop it, take it one step further.

ROBERT A.M. STERN

Stern's characterization aptly describes the second role of study drawings: to provide communication among members of a working group. In all the firms where I conducted interviews, the firm principal, working alone,[7] made a series of initial drawing studies. After pursuing these studies far enough to set a viable direction for the project, the principal gave the original drawings (or copies of them) to one or more assistants from the firm's technical staff, always with verbal instructions about what the assistants were to do. Except for single-person firms or for special projects where the principal designer might continue to work alone, this relation of principal designer to assistants or associates—forming a working group—is typical in contemporary architectural practice.

Thus the transition from private drawing begins with a one-way transmission of graphic and verbal instructions. As the working process continues, graphic and verbal communication broadens from one way to many and reciprocal ways. The drawing's focus changes from a private audience of one to a semi-private audience of two or more collaborators, a change that depends on a core of shared graphic conventions. Through these conventions the principal designer reviews the progress of the work and makes adjustments and corrections to it; or, perhaps, if a major change is needed, makes a whole new drawing. In effect, the principal interprets the drawings produced by someone else, just as one person reads any text written by another. The interpretation is less direct and less continuous than when the principal makes his or her own drawings, but is otherwise similar to the details of interpretation described in chapters 4 and 5.

---

[6]This use of the computer for opening up the design process is discussed further in the appendix of this book.

[7]When Joseph Esherick worked on the two houses discussed in the interview, he made the first several study drawings in meetings with the clients.

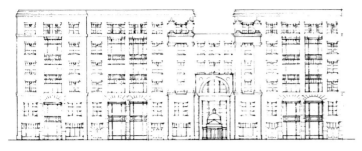

FIGURE 6-6. Robert Stern: base drawing and overlay for New England Life Building, Boston. (Upper) Scale drawing made with straightedge and drawing instruments by technical employee. Hard pencil on heavy tracing paper; 24″ × 15″. Title reads "NEW ENGLAND LIFE / BOYLESTON FACADE / ⅟₁₆″ = 1′-0″ / 15 MAY 87 / RAMS ARCHT." The drawing is well along in the design development sequence. (Lower) Freehand drawings made by Stern on tracing paper laid over the scale drawing. Soft pencil on lightweight tracing paper; central 25″ of a 30″ × 11″ page. Titles under the individual drawings read "Alt 1 . . . Alt 2 . . . Alt 3 . . . Alt 4," starting at the drawing second from the right and going in sequence to the left. The drawings concern the bays with two tall windows symmetrically arranged on each side of the entrance. *Courtesy Robert A.M. Stern Architects.*

An example of the kind of adjustment or corrections a principal designer might make is shown in Stern's tracing paper overlay (figure 6-6). The series of small overlay sketches is intended to study alternative treatments for some part of his assistant's larger drawing. The results of Stern's study would likely be new instruction to his assistant to incorporate one of the alternatives shown on the overlay.

That Stern's small drawings are elevations is obvious as long as the overlay is physically in place on top of its parent elevation drawing, but some additional explanation might be needed if the drawings were separated. Stern would need to identify the small drawings as

alternative elevations. Thus the drawing's graphic conventions permit a designer to talk to someone else about even a very rough separate drawing with only a brief preface to frame the discussion. Such a preface as "this is a section through the auditorium" might be needed, for example, for an assistant to interpret Alvar Aalto's now-separate sketch for the Vuoksenniska Church (figure 6-7)—a drawing so ambiguous that it might be read either as a plan or as a section.

The role of these semi-private drawings is to enable communication within a working group. As the following examples from practice will show, the graphic conventions are not themselves a topic of discussion; they

FIGURE 6-7. Alvar Aalto: section through auditorium, Vuoksenniska church, Imatra, Finland, about 1954. *Courtesy of Student Publications, North Carolina State University.*

are assumed as a basis for the work, not only as given but as transparent.

WORKING WITH OTHERS: EXAMPLES FROM PRACTICE

The discussion above has established that a study drawing by itself is insufficient for communication between individuals working together in design. Some form of spoken or written dialogue is required to complete the context for continued development. Esherick commented on this relation of drawings and dialogue:

> **JE:** If I [am working with someone else], I may do another drawing over the top in order to be more explicit about some of the ideas and because if the person himself hasn't been sitting in on the meeting, they may not understand the intent. Pretty soon, I'll have somebody sit in with me and then they can just pick it up.

> **DH:** So you can't take one of these drawings and put it on someone's desk and say "go"?

> **JE:** Not with any expectation that they will mysteriously understand it.

> **DH:** Do you ever work over other people's drawings, like your giving a drawing to someone else who works with it, and then you draw over it again in a kind of graphic dialogue?

> **JE:** Yes, this next project I'll show you has a lot more of that. . . . [Note: these drawings were not discussed in the interview.]

I asked Stern about the timing of the transition between his own conceptual drawings and the interactions with others:

> **DH:** I understand there's an interchange between you and your assistants; does that begin immediately or do you carry the project through the beginning sequence by yourself?

> **RS:** Basically I would say it begins pretty immediately because I want the person who will be my collaborator, if you will, on any project to be involved from the beginning. I do believe in collaboration; it might be because I'm so secure or so egotistical, whatever.

Stern does not always bring in his collaborators immediately, however, as shown by his earlier account of his first drawings for the U.S. Embassy annex in Budapest (figure 4-13). Tigerman also emphasized the collaboration needed first between principal and assistant, and then between the architectural designers and a separate consultant working with them on the project:

> **ST:** I will sit with Melanie, for example, on a project, and draw in a certain way, and suggest that this or that be done, and then she'll counter and say, "What about this, because that's not so great." The drawings are a vehicle for interaction, more than words, because architects are generally less verbal, so they communicate with each other through their drawings. If more than one architect works on a project . . . in this case it's Melanie and me working on the Palm Beach [project]—whatever she and I work on in this office together—

she's involved, so the best way we can talk to each other, often, is through drawings—not always, because we do understand English, but we express ideas in drawings.

DH: As you are drawing together, you are also talking together, you're adding some context to the drawing.

ST: Here, for example [Tigerman refers to a landscape architect's drawing (figure 1-19)]: it's a small thing, it's not whether I did the drawing or Melanie did the drawing or whatever, but for example on this site plan, there had been some discussion about locating the road, now with the landscape architect. And so we're trying to show on the drawing where the entrance should be, so he has one location which then Melanie has taken from his drawing, and then this is my drawing, I think, and I said, "No, why don't we do this, why don't we curve it in another way?"

All three of these architects have evolved similar ways of working with their employees, attempting to keep them as fully informed and as fully involved as possible. Taking a different approach on the Cincinnati DAAP project (figure 4-10), Peter Eisenman withheld information from his design staff:

PE: I never showed this drawing to my workers for the first two months they were working on the project. I let them make their own drawings.

DH: Then you respond to their drawings based on what you know from these drawings?

PE: I will respond to their drawings, until this reaches a point of exhaustion; I was testing their drawings against these drawings in a certain way.

DH: Were they aware of that?

PE: You could ask them . . . I don't know.

With still another approach, Helmut Jahn, after exploring initial directions on his own, continues to use his drawings primarily as a one-way—or at least unequal—communication channel throughout the development of each project. This kind of operation seems difficult enough to sustain for a few moderate-sized projects; to do it for many large projects at the same time, and to do

it at the detail apparent in the drawings, seems truly remarkable. Keith Palmer, the general manager of the firm, described Jahn's use of drawing as a basis for working with his staff:

DH: Is this all one-way communication: his notion transmitted to the team [i.e., a small working group] and the team follows up?

KP: In the majority, yes, one-way. But again, this process of putting one's pen hand to paper, the same thing follows throughout the team. Sometimes the project architect will say, "Helmut, this doesn't work, but look, we changed this and we did this to it." And he will say, "That works" or "That doesn't work." But the basic ideas and development that he wants are generated by Helmut. Sometimes the team comes up with some adjustment. He will meet with every team every day, more so in the design phase. During the entire life of the project he will keep track of it, go out and come back with changes that he hopes will make it a better building. I say he never leaves a project, he's always going back to it, seeing that it's going in the directions he's established, but he's not unwilling to change it during the process.

DH: Between Helmut's original drawings and these finished drawings were there lots of yellow sketchpaper drawings?

KP: There's not that much yellow trace. Helmut's sketches are really transposed, once distances are established.

DH: I'm beginning to understand that those sketches are so densely packed with information that the job of the team is to read it out and put it down.

KP: Right . . . or it's changed. He will again meet with the project architect every day, to see if everything is going according to the intent of the sketches.

DH: What form do the corrections take? Yellow sketch overlays?

KP: Typically more sketches [i.e., by Jahn]. The majority of [Jahn's] sketches are 4¼ by 5½ inches, which is one-quarter of 8½ by 11 inches. On [the] American [Airlines project],

because of the size of the building, in order to
put any detail on it, he has gone to full 8½ by
11 inches or 8½ inches square. Then they will
start drawing up these elements: sometimes
he's dealing with the connections on this truss
which spans this 300-foot vaulted space, the
infilling of the truss members. He will have
worked on that the previous night, some
element that he wants to develop more and he
will send that to the project architect, or meet
with him and he will say, "I want to change
this."

Jahn's directive approach to working with others
in the firm appears in marked contrast to Esherick's,
Tigerman's, and Stern's efforts to bring their assistants
along as collaborators, and to Eisenman's deliberate
hindering of full communication. Jahn did acknowledge the participation of his employees, however, perhaps as respondents rather than collaborators:

HJ: In the best case, the drawing is an instigation
toward the next step, and what the things look
like at the end, the things always change.
Sometimes the second-, third-generation
drawings, they're only made because somebody
else did another drawing after I made the
initial sketch.

It appears from these examples that the transition
of study drawings from private to semi-private occurs
easily enough. The reliable core of graphic conventions
and the customs of the drafting room allow these architects to focus their attention on the design task rather
than on the system of communication that supports it.
Yet problems in reading drawings do occur.

WORKING WITH OTHERS: MISTAKES AND MISUNDERSTANDINGS

One way to understand how a system works is to see
how it fails. During some of the interviews, I brought up
questions about mistakes and misunderstandings that
can occur when working with others in design. Esherick
was first:

DH: Let's say you had somebody from your staff
who sat through a meeting and then you give
him a drawing to work out. . . . What kinds of
misunderstandings occur?

JE: Probably he'll get too rigid, he may copy it too
exactly. I may draw, for example, on this thing
something that looks like the kitchen that is a
mile long, a completely goofy kitchen idea that
doesn't really work. There are two things that
can happen: they could assume that I had an
idea that would make it work, so they would
draw it the way I drew it and that would be
incorrect; the other thing is that I may have
had an idea and didn't tell them about it and
they had a different idea and tried to make it
work—and sometimes it could be better.

Here Esherick's observation that sometimes misunderstandings may be constructive recalls the earlier
discussion of uncertainty: unforeseen contributions to
the design task. Stern, however—although he had earlier acknowledged the value of working with others—
did not view misunderstandings as useful parts of the
work:

DH: There are lots of life situations when things
don't work, as you said. Can you give me
an example of a time when someone
misunderstood your directions?

RS: Well, when you're working with somebody,
and think the drawing is absolutely clear and
then they can't figure out what to do; then
there's the other thing where people start out
with, say, an elevation and I say, "Let's make a
model of it," and they start worrying about
where are the three other sides of the building
and then change the elevation in order to
make the other three things happen and the
thing I started with gets eroded. That's when I
start a screaming fit, I say, "First we'll finish
that elevation, then we'll see the problems in
the three other sides, but for now this drawing
is the law."

Jahn seemed resigned to mistakes and misunderstandings as a consequence of the density of information in his drawings (figure 6-8):

DH: Are there any cases where your drawings just
don't work, where your staff misunderstands a
drawing?

HJ: Oh yes, people sometimes get tired looking at
those sketches, because nobody likes to be

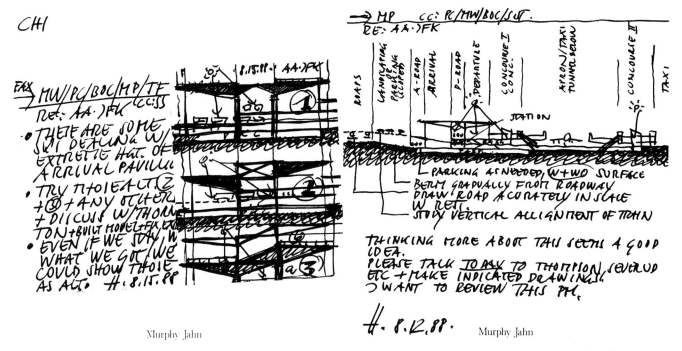

FIGURE 6-8. Helmut Jahn: schematic study drawings for the American Airlines terminal, John F. Kennedy Airport, New York, August 1988. The two drawing pages are mounted together on one album page. Ink on bond paper; 8½″ × 8½″. The initials in upper left corner of each page shows who is supposed to receive a copy of the drawing; the written notes, in addition to explaining aspects of the design, instruct the recipients about what Jahn wants them to do and when he wants to review the results of their work. *Courtesy Helmut Jahn.*

told too many things. So, sometimes people don't see all the little notes, or they pretend they can't read them, or they don't want to read them. Architects want to have, you know . . . [trails off].

It appears that none of these misunderstandings would occur if the architect could continue his work entirely alone; they are all misunderstood intentions about what the principal wanted his assistant to do, not differences of opinion about design issues. Only Esherick acknowledged a possible advantage from a misunderstanding; the others appeared to regard mistakes and misunderstandings as normal but unwelcome noise to be expected in complex communications.

That none of the misunderstandings involved graphic conventions indicates how well these conventions function, how transparent they seem to the participants in the working process. Graphic conventions and the customs of working process function well because they have evolved together in practice and teaching. They accommodate each other so that conventions appear problematic only as a theoretical point, not as a practical matter in getting things done. This is, perhaps, just another way of saying that designers mostly attempt to

do those things that can be expedited by graphic conventions.

Expediting things is no small matter, however, in the complexities of architectural practice. For design to go forward, there must be some way for the information developed through design study drawings to become progressively more public, for private drawings to become semi-private within a working group, for semi-private drawings of the working group to become semi-public and then fully public as the working process widens. Thus it is essential that the same core of graphic conventions that frames the individual designer's solitary thoughts also develops them into solid proposals and communicates them to an external audience of clients and builders.

REFERENCES

Eco, Umberto. 1980. Function and sign: the semiotics of architecture. In *Signs, Symbols and Architecture,* ed. Geoffrey Broadbent, Richard Bunt, and Charles Jencks, pp. 33-67. Chichester: John Wiley and Sons.

Jurgens, Hartmut, Heinz-Otto Peitgen, and Dietmar Saupe. 1990. The language of fractals. *Scientific American* (August): 60-67.

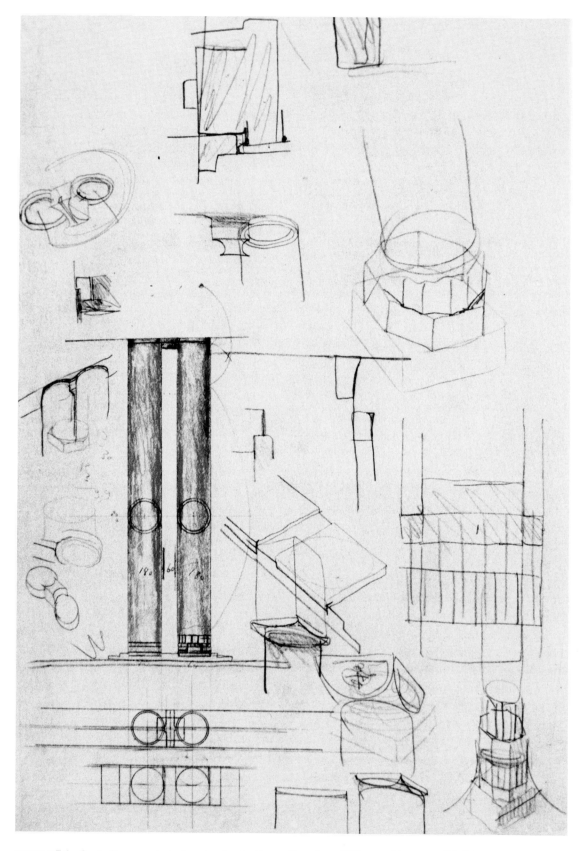

FIGURE 7-1. Carlo Scarpa: study drawing for the Banca Popolare di Verona, Verona, 1973. Black and colored pencil on thin cardboard; 300mm × 600mm (about 12″ × 24″), shown cropped to 425mm. The original drawing was at a scale of 1:25, or about ½″ = 1′-0″. *Courtesy Archivio Scarpa.*

WATCHING SCARPA DRAW:
A RECONSTRUCTION

Carlo Scarpa began his study of paired interior columns slightly to the left of center on a cream-colored board about 12 inches wide and 24 inches high. Working with pencil, straightedge, and scale he drew an accurate elevation of two column shafts (figure 7-1).[1] In careful freehand, he added a stepped base at the bottom of the columns, then with a compass drew circular sections of the column shafts at their midheight. As he drew these sections, he realized that the columns were too far apart, so he marked a reduced spacing with short freehand lines alongside the columns on the elevation and noted not only the changed space between the columns (60) but also the unchanged dimension of the column shafts (180). Using his straightedge and compass again, he drew plan sections—including a false start that had to be erased—of the column base and capital (lower left), showing the reduced spacing. Next he sketched in some simple bands—again with the straightedge—at the top and bottom of the elevation to suggest base and capital moldings, and he added red color to the column shafts. With other freehand sketches, including sections, elevations, and perspectives scattered about the page, he explored possible treatments for the column base and capital: he investigated a variety of whole and partial fluting schemes concerning the column bases (lower and upper right); he searched for some new approach to the column capitals, jotting down an abstracted Romanesque block capital[2] as a reference for three possible modifications (lower center and right), all abandoned in favor of a recessed capital with a spacer block (left); he explored possible construction details for the recessed capital (upper left and center) and base (lower right), and he returned to the elevation drawing to try out the ones that interested

---

[1]The sequence described in the text is inferred from the graphic evidence on the page, from my own drawing practice, and from observing students and employees at work. For example, Scarpa must have drawn the elevation/plan group first: it is inconceivable that a designer would draw a group of randomly located freehand sketches and leave just enough space to draw a set of scaled elevation and plans.

---

[2]The Romanesque capital appears to be a drawing made to recall the image out of Scarpa's long-term memory and to bring it into the current design task, similar to the drawing Stanley Tigerman made of the cloister plan described in chapter 6. Scarpa's capital is also similar to Tigerman's cloister in that they are both abstracted types rather than particular instances.

7

CONTINUITY
AND CHANGE

him. Finally, at the top of the page, he turned his attention to another subject unrelated to the columns, drawing what appears to be two door frame detail sections. Apparently Scarpa found no reason to challenge any graphic conventions in his work: these sketches all read as straightforward plan, elevation, section, perspective, or axonometric drawings.

An overview of the whole page shows two types of drawings: first, the grouped elevation and plan sections showing the whole column assembly to scale; and second, the fragmented, unscaled sketches scattered about in locations determined by circumstance.

It seems clear that Scarpa had dissimilar intentions for these two drawing types: the larger elevation/plan group was begun first—no doubt based on information from some earlier study—to show the general spatial order of the current design task, while the scattered smaller section, elevation, and perspective drawings were made later, are graphically more fragmented and abstract, and are intended to explore possible changes in issues selected from the context of the larger drawings. In the working process, the larger context drawings provide a home base for the comings and goings of the smaller exploration drawings. In short, the larger drawing provides continuity; the exploration drawings provide change. These two complementary kinds of drawing are so characteristic of study drawings that they form the basis for a statement of study drawing's fifth epistemological property: *study drawings provide both continuity and change within a dynamic working process.*

I will begin the examination of this property by analyzing the working process in some detail. The concepts brought forward in earlier chapters having to do with pre-existing order, the cyclic interaction of graphics and cognition, and the effects of graphic conventions make it possible now to go beyond static descriptions of the working process and consider it as a dynamic system.

DYNAMICS OF THE WORKING PROCESS

How does the working process introduce change into the design task so that the work can advance? Charles Rusch's description of continual mental restructuring suggests a source for change:

> The [short-term] memory structure is by no means static or rigid; it is dynamic and constantly

undergoing modifications during recall when it is fed back through the constructive activity of immediate experience. On each recycle the structure is rebuilt, new information is added, parts of the old structure are discarded, while other parts are changed only indirectly by the changes in the context which surrounds them. (Rusch 1970, 63)

This dynamic description of cognitive structures neatly fits the working process in design: images from memory are triggered by elements that have been abstracted from initial statements about the program, site, and surroundings. These early images provide a new structural base for including further information from the designer's long-term memory and from new data about the design task. Still more complex imaginal structures build up through progressive cycles as the design develops. From this description, it might seem that an experienced designer could gather and study all the data about a project, think through the design, and begin making the final drawings. The graphic evidence noted in chapter 4 shows that designers do not work that way, however, and there is reason to believe that designers *cannot* work that way.

The reason why designers cannot think through design issues entirely in their minds is that the human cognitive and visual systems can carry only a limited amount of image-based information at any one time. In an essay on the psychology of communication, George Miller (1967) observes that "... there is a finite span of immediate memory and that for a lot of different kinds of test materials this span is about seven items in length" (25), and that "we can [only] make relatively crude judgments of several things simultaneously" (29).[3] These limits on mental processing confirm the observation noted in chapter 4 that whatever mental images designers may have are neither clear enough nor complete enough to carry on the design task without the aid of

---

[3]Miller's classic essay entitled "The Magical Number Seven, Plus or Minus Two: Some Limits on Our Capacity for Processing Information," from which the two quotations were taken, originally appeared in *Psychological Review* 1956, 63, p. 93. The essay summarizes research related to the information-processing capacities of the human brain and offers new conclusions on the subject. The essay still appears as a datum for recent research, such as the study by Nicolis and Tsuda (1985). These authors propose a dynamic model of information processing that they say can "reproduce the 'magic number seven plus-minus two' and also its variance in a number of cases and provide a theoretical justification for them" (343).

study drawings. So, as mental images become more complex in the working process, it becomes necessary to rely on drawings as a memory annex to carry the overloads, to permit designers to catch, save, reinterpret, and build on those increments of new information that are introduced from memory or perception. Study drawings supply this memory annex, or external storage, providing continuity for the evolving design task.

Storage is too static a term, however. Complementing cognitive processes in an evolving design requires the external storage system to change, and change quickly. Observation as well as introspection suggests that, aside from short-term variations, there is a general rhythm or pace to developmental change in design work, and that an uninterrupted flow of this change is more effective than an interrupted or impeded one. Quickness in making study drawings is needed not to save what could be only a few minutes for some other activity, but to keep up the pace of change in the work, to capture as much as possible from the continuous reinterpretation of the cognitive image as it builds in new aspects of the design task.

How can study drawings complement such dynamic cognitive processes? Can other parts of the working process support this pace? In practice, designers intuitively make their working process more effective by speeding up their architectural study drawings. Their techniques for drawing quickly can be understood by means of concepts from studies in graphics and from psychological studies in visual perception.

Graphic techniques are the most obvious. Scarpa's drawing of the columns (figure 7-1) and Louis I. Kahn's study plan (figure 7-2) show several ways to economize drawing time, all made possible because these are private drawings intended to be read only by their authors.

MINIMIZING UNNECESSARY SYMBOLS AND NOTATION

Neither Scarpa's nor Kahn's drawings show any conventional architectural symbols. They do not show what materials are being considered (except, perhaps, Scarpa's scribbled hatching in the door frame detail); Kahn's plan shows no conventional door swing symbols; Scarpa's dimensions are jotted in, without dimension lines, arrows, or witness lines; neither Scarpa's nor Kahn's drawings are titled or given a scale notation. Since the study drawing is, in the first instance, always a private drawing, it does not need the symbols and notations that a public drawing does. Such notations are either irrelevant to the designer's purpose in early drawings (such as Kahn's) or easily assumed by their author in later ones (such as Scarpa's).

CUTTING DOWN ON DETAIL

Experienced designs often omit detail. Both Scarpa's and Kahn's exploration drawings show only a limited subject for study: where Scarpa thinks about the form of the top shoulder of the column, he draws only the essence of its section (center); where Kahn wants to study the massing of parts of the plan, he draws only generalized square forms (lower right). Scarpa's context drawing of the column elevation shows the most detail of these examples. Since the purpose of the drawing is to explore the details of the column's form, a large scale and a certain amount of detail are necessary; but Scarpa does not include any detail of the column's connection to floor or ceiling or its internal construction. Kahn's context drawing, made at a much earlier stage of his work, is clearly about the general formal organization of the project, so he does not try to show details of openings, structure, or room arrangements. On the plan at the left, where he is apparently concerned with the relationship of the two symmetrical masses, he shows only the merest squiggle to represent a generalized idea of enclosure for the rest of the walls.

ACCEPTING ROUGH DRAWINGS AS FINISHED

For their own studies, experienced designers feel no obligation to make finished drawings. Although Scarpa's context drawing shows that he can make a finished drawing when he wants to, his exploration drawings are graphically informal. The exploration drawings show that he made no effort to straighten lines or to keep drawings aligned (upper right) or to complete drawings in which he had lost interest (left side, just below center). Even rougher are Kahn's drawings, including both the context drawing and the exploration drawings. These drawings are so unfinished that their specific intent is literally unintelligible to others, and possibly unintelligible even to Kahn himself at some later time.

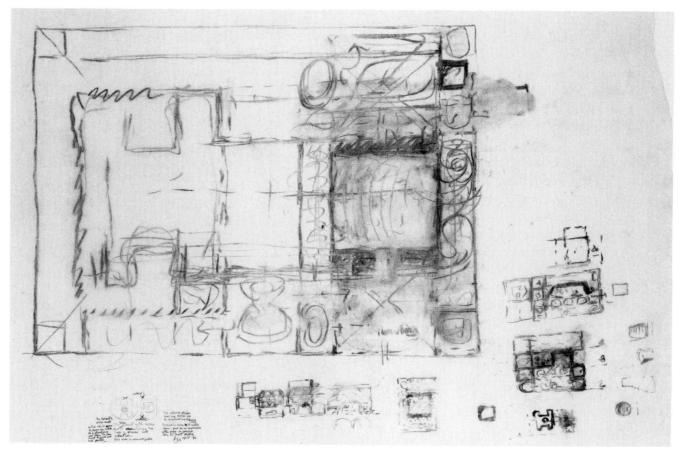

FIGURE 7-2. Louis I. Kahn: plan and section studies for the Yale Center for British Art, New Haven, Connecticut, April 1970. Charcoal on yellow tracing paper; about 18″ × 12″. The small drawing at lower center is a section; the group of notes and diagrams at lower left appears to be in pencil, probably added after the charcoal drawing. *Copyright 1977. Louis I. Kahn collection, University of Pennsylvania and Pennsylvania Historical and Museum Commission.*

MAKING DRAWINGS THE RIGHT SIZE

Studies in the psychology of visual perception suggest reasons why designers intuitively prefer small exploration drawings for most of their work. A small drawing (figure 7-3) is not only physically faster to make,[4] but studies in the psychology of perception suggest that the visual system processes a small drawing more efficiently than a large one. That is, a small drawing allows more of the drawing to be held in the central area of the eye's retina, where visual receptors are concentrated; this central area may be functionally defined as the useful

field of view (UFV).[5] The UFV varies according to the complexity of the background, but for moderately complex fields such as Scarpa's drawing, the UFV might be about 6 degrees. A 6-degree angle at a normal viewing (and drawing) distance of about 18 inches would suggest an image of about 2 inches'

---

[4]My informal observation of drawings by some of my students suggests that the time it takes to make a given drawing is directly proportional not to the area of the drawing but to the number of hand positions required.

[5]Haber and Hershenson (1980) note that ". . . the size of the useful field of view [may be defined] as the area surrounding the fixation point from which the perceiver can detect, discriminate, process, or store information during a given visual task. . . . The useful field of view is about 6 degrees for targets of this size embedded in similar background items. Had the targets been larger or the context items less similar, the useful field of view would undoubtedly have been larger" (328). They continue by saying that "too much information causes their field to constrict so as to prevent overloading the processing system. Adding visual noise or unwanted signals can narrow this useful field of view, creating what Mackworth calls tunnel vision—a priority given to targets in the fovea. There is even some loss in foveal recognition" (329).

FIGURE 7-3. Author: part of a page of graphic notes from a desk critique with student, May 1986. Light pencil on lightweight tracing paper; $10'' \times 8''$. Shown actual size; part of a $10'' \times 14''$ original. *Courtesy Daniel Herbert.*

diameter to fill the UFV. In Scarpa's drawing, the large "elevation" exploration drawing at the right is about 3 inches wide by 4 inches high; the Romanesque capital drawing is about 2 inches by 2 inches. This difference in size suggests the sequence of drawings: Scarpa may have made the larger of these two drawings early on, before the page became cluttered, and thus he worked with a large UFV of about 10 degrees; and he may have made the smaller drawing later when the fuller page reduced the UFV to 6 degrees. Furthermore, a drawing of a size that expresses one idea and can be held as a whole in the UFV has a cognitive advantage: it allows concentration on the idea without the distraction of having to shift the UFV from one place to another in a diffuse and usually cluttered visual field. Concentrating is more efficient than

searching. The designer's intuitive response to the need for speed and small size accounts for the ubiquitous small exploration drawings located as graphic asides at the margins of the larger context drawings. These graphic asides permit study of a particular part of the primary drawing without losing track of the context by turning to another page.

Surprisingly, the relation of drawing size to the UFV holds even for Le Corbusier's large charcoal sketch (figure 4-6). This is an arm-and-hand drawing in an uncluttered visual field, implying a viewing and drawing distance of about 30 inches (that is, arm's length) and a UFV of 8 to 10 degrees. These data suggest an image of about 5 inches in diameter, which accords well with the observed central figure—the building plan—of the drawing.

Besides these specific graphic techniques for drawing quickly, experienced designers share a common approach to the pace of the working process: they draw and think steadily. For example, the interview with Joseph Esherick quoted in chapter 4 noted that the drawing in figure 4-9 took about eight to nine minutes and that he evidently did not have some mental image to record. During this time Esherick drew steadily and quickly not just because of his skill but also because he knew what his design task was, what he wanted to do with the drawing. Earlier in the interview, the issue of understanding the design task had come up in connection with the scale of design drawings:

DH: When [a design task] has a lot of known items in it, then you want a scale that will hold them. In the winery project there's no point in worrying at ⅛-inch scale because you don't have the information to put into it; here on the house you do. I often see students start designing at ¼-inch scale and they don't have any idea what to draw; the paper seems enormous.

JE: Yes, that's an important point. People often ask, "What's blocking students, why don't they do more?" They don't do more because they don't know what to do, and what they need to ask themselves is, "How am I going to solve this particular problem right here?" Maybe they have a detail situation — how does the door sill work? I think trying to figure out how you're going to do it helps enormously in clarifying what you're up to. They don't know how to draw a wall section because they've never thought through a wall section. I think your comment about not having enough information to put into that scale is a very good way to put it.

From his experience in making architectural drawings for about 50 years, Esherick has learned the nature of the design task, not just in familiar situations concerning wall sections and door sills but in new situations concerning unfamiliar assemblies. This intuitive sense of what is needed and how to get it enables him to find a constructive approach to a design task and to keep up a steady pace of drawing and thinking.

Helmut Jahn also commented on the pace of drawing and on the relation of mind to hand:

DH: Give me an idea about how long it would take you to make a drawing. Here are two drawings [dated] 12/10/88 for JFK (figure 1-18); on the right-hand drawing it looks like a couple of sections and some notes. . . . How long does it take to do a drawing like that?

HJ: Those two sheets, maybe ten minutes. . . .

DH: The more detailed drawings, are those also very fast sketches?

HJ: Yes . . . some of the time. . . .

DH: Do you think your mind is going faster than the drawing; is your hand keeping up with your mind?

HJ: I think it's a mutual thing, the hand just goes automatically. That's why I say the drawing you do in agony, in the search, you do better drawings because you're not conscious that you make a drawing.

Peter Eisenman also had a sense of the time it took to make his drawings: in response to a question about his first conceptual drawings for the University of Cincinnati DAAP project he replied, "Yes, they're fast, maybe I was drawing for an hour or so." These conceptual drawings were on three pages (figure 4-10, shows one of the three) containing about 16 to 18 plan studies; to have done all of these in "an hour or so" would mean drawing at a pace of one plan study about every four minutes.

Some preliminary observations can be made even from these meager data about these designers' drawing pace. Taking the eight- to nine-minute total time for Esherick's drawing (figure 4-9) as given and assuming that Jahn's and Eisenman's time estimates are realistic, these times conform roughly to David Ullman's video-taped protocols of experienced engineering designers making study drawings, but suggest more variations in pace than Ullman found (Ullman, Wood, and Craig 1990). The marks in architectural drawings appear to be considerably more ambiguous and perhaps more numerous than those in Ullman's study, so his results cannot be transferred directly to architectural design except to observe that it appears that experienced architectural designers do draw rapidly and could only have time for brief pauses between blocks of drawing activity.[6] This finding confirms in general that drawing and thinking are not separate activities in architectural design: one would not find experienced designers spending much time looking away from their drawing boards and "thinking"; rather, they spend most of their time drawing. For them, drawing—with its concurrent interpretation—is thinking.

THE WORKPLACE

Strictly graphic techniques that maintain the pace of the work are often supplemented by another intuitively organized part of the working process: the physical workplace. The architectural workplace typically reflects the need for fast changes and getting information quickly. Here, completed study drawings and other visual references are kept available in a changing array; casually pinned up, overlaid, and scattered about in apparent confusion.

The workplace is not as confused as it seems, however, because it provides a short-term pool of stored images to back up the active role of the study drawings (Stoker and Weingarten 1983). The designer's memory "map" of the location of various drawings and other images in the workplace allows him or her to make a directed search of the workplace (figure 7-4). In this directed search, the designer's perceptual system anticipates reaching its target and recaptures a needed element almost instantly as it reaches the center of the

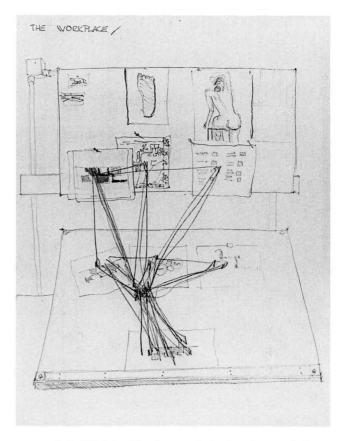

FIGURE 7-4. Miltiades Mandros: analysis of student workplace, Department of Architecture, University of Oregon, January 1990. Pencil on bond paper; 8½″ × 11″. Mandros's drawing records his own changing focus of visual attention while working on design. *Courtesy Miltiades Mandros.*

useful field of view.[7] Because this mental map is personal, one person's casual order may be someone else's mess. An excerpt from the interview with Robert Stern deals with this point:

RS: I don't like to work at someone else's desk, because that's their mess and I start tidying it. I get distracted by the mess on their desk.

---

[6]Ullman identified design "episodes" of about a minute long within the working process. In each episode, a designer typically made about eight marks on the page with pauses of about one second or less between marks and longer pauses between episodes. Each episode satisfied a primitive goal, such as "find a way to mount the arm to the frame." Esherick's drawing (figure 4-9) that took about eight to nine minutes has about 50 marks, or an average of about five to six per minute—a little less than the eight that Ullman found. Eisenman's drawings show between about 20 (low) and 60 marks (high), with an average of about 40 for each plan. This suggests about ten marks per minute for a four-minute plan, or a little faster than Ullman found. Jahn's drawings show about 400 to 500 marks (including each letter in his written notes as a mark); in ten minutes, as reported, this would be 40 to 50 per minute, or more than five times Ullman's reported rate—high enough to suppose that Jahn may have underestimated the time to make the two drawings. It is also likely that my inclusion of Jahn's extensive written notes has distorted the count. These averages are very rough both in time and mark counts but, except for Jahn's report, they indicate general conformance with Ullman's taped protocols.

---

[7]Haber and Hershenson (1980) describe the mechanics of the directed search: "The functional fovea is like a zoom lens . . . which can be widened or narrowed depending upon the task. The first few glances of a scene may be made in a wide-angle fovea useful in picking up the prominent features, but not being able to resolve much detail. After the gist of the scene is acquired, then the foveal field of view narrows and fine detail is examined piece by piece" (335). "Mere overlap isn't usually sufficient for integration to occur. Instead, . . . the perceiver constructs a schematic map . . . that consists of a set of cognitive expectancies about what has already been seen [peripherally] and what will be seen if the fovea is shifted to a new place on the stimulus" (341).

FIGURE 7-5. Drafting desks of technical employees in Stern's office (left) and Tigerman's office (right). *Photo by Daniel Herbert.*

DH: I assume your own desk is just as messy as anyone else's. . . .

RS: No, I am a tidy person; I like a clean surface to work on. I might make a messy drawing, but I like to do it on a clean surface. The rest of the office is a complete mess, but not my desk.

DH: And when you work at this clean desk are there reference materials around?

RS: Oh yes, you would put the building or drawings or whatever right there.

Stern's desk might appear cluttered to someone else who did not share his mental map of the references he was using at a given time. Whatever idiosyncrasies the principals may have had, however, work stations in all the firms represented in the interviews were about the same: drafting desks were characteristically cluttered, with variations according to personal taste and drafting room policies (figure 7-5).[8]

Some designers redefine the workplace to make it portable. By means of sketchbooks and their skill in freehand drawing, both Jahn and Tigerman keep working even while traveling. Both also commented on the use of FAX as a means of extending the workplace beyond its traditional confines. Although neither Kahn

nor Le Corbusier had access to FAX, sketchbooks are not new: Kahn's sketchbooks are well known, and Le Corbusier made many of his drawings for Ronchamp in the sketchbooks he almost always carried with him (figure 7-6). The sketchbook combines the working medium, memory annex, and archive in a single format.

Thus the workplace as well as the working process must provide both continuity and change. The design task requires designers not only to manipulate complex and changeable patterns of graphic symbols, but also to fix certain aspects of those patterns as a basis for further evolution. This requirement, combined with the limitations of human mental processes, demands an external storage system that can change even as it holds the design task together in space and time. The typical external storage system—now almost exclusively a circumstantial pencil-and-paper contraption—is embedded in a working process that has its own pace, determined by interactions between the graphic storage system and the dynamic cognitive processes it supports.

Understanding the working process and the workplace provides a basis to consider context and exploration drawings in more detail. I will first describe how these two types of drawings are sometimes combined and then examine their separate but complementary functions.

COMBINED CONTEXT AND EXPLORATION DRAWINGS

The earliest drawings for a design, such as Le Corbusier's charcoal sketch of June 6, 1950 (figure 3-1), commonly

[8]Designers need the display space provided by tackable enclosure surface. An acquaintance in a firm whose principal was not interviewed for this study reported that the firm's "clean-desk" policy in the drafting room caused a substantial amount of interruption to consult out-of-sight references that she would have preferred to have out on her desk or pinned up for ready viewing.

combine the functions of context and exploration drawings. The design task starts with a relatively simple drawing (figure 4-7) that does not immediately generate a body of decisions large enough to require a separate context drawing. As the designer's investigation continues, it is possible to conduct explorations directly on the early drawing. The building plan starts as an exploration drawing and then becomes a combined context and exploration drawing.

At a simpler level, some design tasks stay small. Each of Tigerman's studies for money clips (figure 7-7), for example, can be held as a whole in the designer's short-term memory so that only exploration drawings are needed.

The page of drawings by Alvar Aalto for the Vuoksenniska Church (figure 7-8) appears, like Tigerman's, to be made up only of exploration drawings, but the variety of subjects suggests that it probably refers to a context drawing on a separate page. Although the drawing is not dated in relation to other drawings for the project, it is clear that these detailed explorations belong to a complex project already so well developed that it could not be held as a whole in the designer's memory.

Thus context and exploration drawings may be combined for early and simple tasks, but later editions of study drawings for complex tasks typically show graphically distinct roles for context and exploration drawings. The existence of these complementary but separate roles raises questions about specific details of the working processs: How do context drawings maintain continuity as the design task gets more complex, and how can they represent something that does not yet exist? How do exploration drawings introduce change into the design task, how do they produce new meanings, and what makes a good exploration drawing?

CONTEXT DRAWINGS

Context drawings show the current design task as a whole, usually at some conventional scale. Examples of context drawings include Scarpa's column elevation (figure 7-1), Kahn's plan for the Yale Center for British Art (figure 7-2), Bramante's plan for St. Peter's (figure 2-6), Scarpa's perspective (figure 7-9), Aalto's plan of the Helsinki Concert Hall (figure 7-10), and Keller's roof plan for the McMinnville Library (figure 1-3). These examples all show a single large context drawing stating the current focus of the design task accompanied by

FIGURE 7-6. Le Corbusier: sketches for chapel at Ronchamp, summer 1950. Ink on 4″ × 6″ page of sketchbook. *From* The Le Corbusier Sketchbooks, *vol. 2. Copyright: Architectural History Foundation and MIT Press. Sketchbook #D-17. Reproduced by permission of MIT Press.*

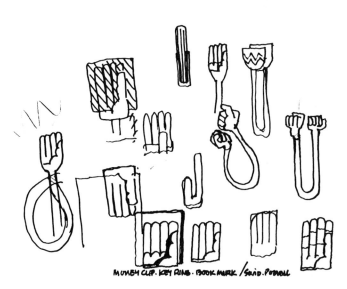

FIGURE 7-7. Stanley Tigerman: sketches for money clips, key rings, and book marks. Ink on sketchbook page, 8″ × 5″. *Courtesy Tigerman McCurry Architects.*

exploration drawings spun off from it. As a design develops, the design task for the whole project gets larger; then several context drawings are required to hold it all—not just one drawing, but a set of them, including plans, elevations, sections, etc.

Whether in one drawing or a set of them, context drawings appear to be straightforward graphic representations of a whole or part of a building—easily assumed to provide transparent access to an external reality as described in chapter 2. Under this assumption,

FIGURE 7-8. Alvar Aalto: local and global studies for Vuoksenniska church, Imatra, Finland, about 1954. *Reproduced from* Alvar Aalto: Synopsis, *edited by Bernhard Hoesli, published by Birkhauser Verlag, Basel, 1970.*

design context drawings are very much like drawings of completed buildings found in history books—say, for St. Paul's Cathedral (figure 7-11). Viewers of such drawings normally assume the possibility of matching one-to-one points of correspondence between the drawing and the building, and can test this assumption by taking the drawing to London and, allowing for certain graphic conventions, seeing how well it matches the building.

Although matching corresponding points may be one way to test a drawing of an existing building, it cannot serve as a test for a context drawing. A context drawing such as Aalto's plan of the Helsinki Concert Hall (figure 7-10) is very unlike the plan of St. Paul's. For Aalto—as for any designer—the current context drawing (or a set of them) cannot match a building. At the time a context study drawing is made no building exists for it to match.

What does a context drawing match, then? The eventual building? No; the outcome of development is inherently uncertain, so there is no predictable eventual building to serve as a test for matching. The class of buildings that might be developed from the drawing? Meaningless, since an infinite number of dissimilar buildings, or none, might be developed from it. A men-

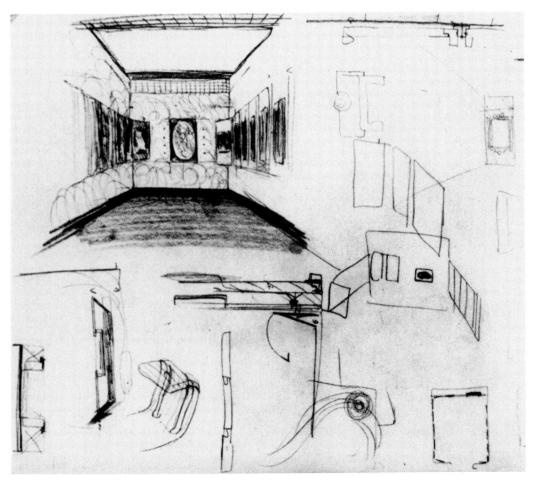

FIGURE 7-9. Carlo Scarpa: studies for a museum installation for the Gallerie dell'Accademia, 1949. Pencil and crayon on tracing paper, 295mm × 452mm (about 11½″ × 17½″). The perspective at upper left serves as a context drawing. Among the exploration drawings, another small perspective drawing at middle right investigates a possible global reorganization of the whole space. *Courtesy Archivio Scarpa.*

FIGURE 7-10. Alvar Aalto: study plan for Helsinki Concert Hall, Helsinki, Finland, 1962. Here Aalto, in struggling with the polygonal plan of the meeting chamber, has overdrawn it several times in its original position until the drawing was illegible and, evidently not yet satisfied, has redrawn the plan below the main drawing. *© 1971 Verlag für Architektur, Artemis Zürich. Alvar Aalto, Werke Band II 1963-1970.*

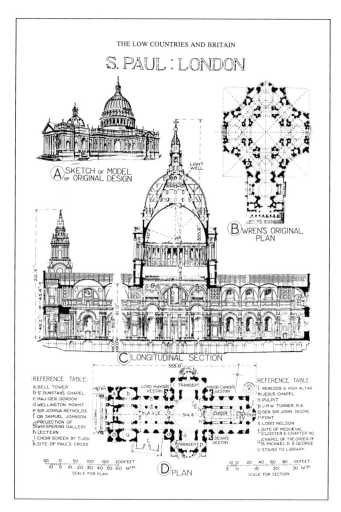

FIGURE 7-11. Drawing from Sir Banister Fletcher's *A History of Architecture,* representing St. Paul's Cathedral, London, England. *From Sir Banister Fletcher's* A History of Architecture, *Courtesy British Architectural Library, RIBA, London.*

tal image? No; the discussion in chapters 4 and 5 has shown that cognitive images are neither clear enough nor complete enough to serve as objects of such complex matchings. Perhaps the drawing matches itself? Perhaps; but the notion is both circular and unnecessary, a product of the tacit assumption that the only representational role of drawings is to match something.

Rather, the context drawing has roles other than matching. It appears from the way designers use these drawings that the context drawing has two representational roles that do not involve matching: holding information in place and managing change.

The designer uses the context drawing to hold in place all the information made through previous decisions: information about the sizes and shapes of the materials, assemblies, and connections—a kind of graphic

index of information about the design. The context drawing is more than an index, however, inasmuch as it also holds the general order of spatial, relational, and tractile information, such as proportion, relative size, alignment, or texture. Scarpa's drawing of the columns, for example, not only states his intentions for the base and capital but also states their relative proportion and the distance between them. The context drawing presents all that the designer knows about the work at that stage of the design task—all that can be known. It defines the work. Contemporary British architect Zaha Hadid has said as much regarding her own drawings: "The projection of the architecture becomes the architecture itself."[9] The drawing constitutes the design by holding in place all the information about it.

Holding in place such design information gives continuity to the process of design and construction: it makes realizing a building possible. Realizing a building from a designer's study drawings does not depend just on the designer's own will, however, as might be said of completing a painting or sculpture from an artist's study drawings. In any situation where a designer does not intend to make a proposed building with his or her own hands, realizing a building requires another layer of structure: an institutionalized process that guides the development of any architectural project from beginning to end. Chapter 6 noted that the conventional graphic projections of plan, section, etc., are essential to make study drawings useful during design and construction. Yet graphic projections are not the only conventions built into the whole process. The institutionalized conventions of professional practice and the building industry guide the transition from private to public drawings and assure designers that by following certain rules even the roughest study drawings can eventually lead to a completed building. These rules and conventions control what happens, when it happens, and who does it. Designers learn, for example, that they must revise and extend their first rough sketches before sending them to a builder; that they may defer choosing specific materials until they have defined a project's general schematic organization; that as their drawings get more public, they must consider certain subdivisions of the building industry. Such institutionalized conventions—which are always evolving in response to their own internal and external pressures—impose

[9]Zaha Hadid, quoted in Hatton (1988).

another layer of pre-existing structure on the process even as they provide for the systematic integration of certain kinds of new information.

For well-developed drawings approaching final publication, new information comes from technical sources and operations such as building codes, engineering calculations, data from equipment and material manufacturers, and shop drawings from fabrication contractors. For still-undeveloped study drawings, the new information comes from cycles of exploration drawings.

Cycles of exploration drawings introduce change, and managing this change is the second non-matching role of context drawings. The designer uses the current state of the context drawing as a guide for deciding what exploration studies to make next and then to evaluate the results of those studies. Scarpa's drawing of the columns (figure 7-1) prompts him to investigate the moldings at the column base in a separate drawing, then to draw the results of this investigation into the elevation as shown on the right-hand column, and finally to decide whether they make the column base what it ought to be. And Aalto's plan drawing (figure 7-10) prompts him to move to the lower part of the drawing page to explore another way of ordering the small polygonal meeting hall and then to incorporate his findings in either the parent drawing or its inevitable successor. Exploration drawings introduce change; context drawings manage it.

Thus context drawings do not stand alone. Further understanding of the role of context drawings in managing change requires turning to a detailed discussion of exploration drawings as the source of change in the design task.

EXPLORATION DRAWINGS

In general, progress in the design task occurs when the designer focuses on some selected feature of a design task and explores possible changes in it. The drawings used to explore possible changes are called *exploration drawings*. Exploration drawings often appear as graphic asides at the edges of a context drawing (the small drawings in figures 7-1, 7-2, 7-9, 7-10, 1-3, and 2-6). As an exploration drawing is prompted from its parent context drawing, the information that describes the selected feature is abstracted from its context, its subject is investigated by the exploration drawing, and the result

is returned to be reintegrated into the next edition of the context drawing. On any drawing page, then, the exploration drawings are made later than and are more abstract than the context drawing. This general view provides a basis for understanding exploration drawings in specific detail.

Exploration drawings may investigate issues ranging from local to global: local issues are those concerned with specific parts of the design task, and global issues are concerned with general aspects. For example, all of Scarpa's exploration drawings in the column study (figure 7-1) are about local issues, about this part or that part of the larger context drawing that shows the column assembly; Kahn's marginal studies explore localized issues abstracted from the context drawing of the two floor plans (figure 7-2); Stern's series of entrance studies are all local issues (figure 6-6). Global exploration studies consider such general issues as axial relationships (figure 7-12), large patterns (central part of figure 7-8), or overall spatial organization (figure 7-9, right central small perspective). Scarpa did not make any global explorations of the column study (figure 7-1); he did not, for example, make some small exploration drawings grouping three columns together or fusing the two columns into an articulated pier. Whatever the focus of the study, local or global, each exploration starts with an act of abstraction, separating the subject from its context.

Abstracting a subject from its context requires several structuring decisions about what part of the context drawing is a significant subject for study, which elements of the subject are essential to the study, how to reorganize them into a coherent whole, and how to restate them in a new format. These decisions have a profound effect on the abstracted subject's design content, because, as the earlier discussion has shown, this manipulation of information involves imposing a particular, and even ideological, structure on it and losing a certain amount of the primary data as the inevitable cost of the subject's attaining its separate identity. Whether it is explicitly selected by redrawing the subject of the study in a separate base drawing (figure 7-7), or implicitly selected by either making an overlay drawing (figures 1-19, 6-6) or focusing attention on one area rather than another as a subject for overdrawing (figure 7-10), it embodies significant design decisions even before it is used for its intended exploration.

Just as the parent context drawing is not a device for matching, neither is the exploration drawing abstracted

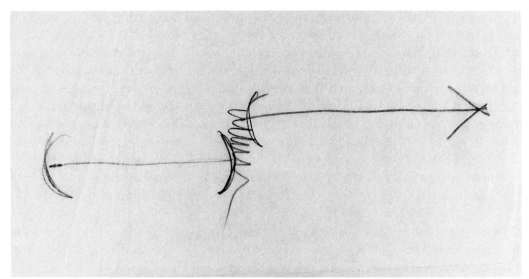

FIGURE 7-12. Author: study of an interrupted axial relationship from a desk critique with student, University of Oregon Department of Architecture, May 1976. Pencil on lightweight tracing paper; $12'' \times 6''$; part of a larger original. *Courtesy Daniel Herbert.*

from it. Where the two non-matching roles of the context drawing are holding in place and managing change, the exploration drawing has its own non-matching role: creating change, or producing new meanings.

How does the exploration drawing produce new meanings? The drawing's meaning is determined neither by matching a part of an external reality, nor, since it has been abstracted, by reference to the context drawing. Rather, the exploration drawing can mean whatever the designer intends it to mean. By being drawn on a page, it is simultaneously a graphic artifact and a cognitive structure that is set in motion through a field of other cognitive structures. It possesses a high potential for connection—for gaining and giving new meanings. It is like a multipoled magnet linking with other magnetized structures in an active field. The drawing carries whatever meanings have been ascribed to it as the designer makes it, but these meanings are not fixed; they are intended to change as described in the discussion of the two key graphic/cognitive interactions for generating information in chapter 5. Thus the same drawing carries back new meanings picked up as the designer forms new cognitive structures through new interpretations.

The cost of the exploration drawing's attaining this free existence is that it has become so abstract that it is purely a graphic mark. In this sense design becomes a purely graphic activity, its marks made and read in the same way that marks of a literary text may be read when words are interpreted not as representations of some external and material objects but as artifacts of language—as texts—whose rules of composition and

interpretation have to do with the internal order of language. Chapter 2 noted that a drawing as a text has its own existence aside from any building it may represent, that it has its own internal rules, and that it can carry meaning. Continuing the quotation from the interview with Eisenman begun in chapter 2 provides a basis for applying this idea of text specifically to exploration drawings:

DH: . . . So the drawing becomes an entity that you read back to yourself. . . .

PE: A true text. It's not the representation of a text, it's the text itself.

DH: Something that Derrida (1977) wrote could be applied to what I believe is going on in study drawings: "[A script, or text] does not exhaust itself in the moment of its inscription." That describes how I understand drawing to work in design: in the act of drawing, we make a text that we then reinterpret and thereby understand more than we have put down. Is that a fair statement?

PE: That's right, rather close. . . . I would say that my drawing is writing, I don't see any difference between them. I write the same way, I write as a stream of consciousness, I don't have any idea what I'm going to write until I start to write.

DH: The writing or the drawing takes on a life of its own and we are there to assist.

Here the passage confirms an earlier point in this book's discussion that designers can read more out of a drawn text—such as an exploration drawing—than they put into it. The passage also extends the idea that the drawing is not limited to representing something else; it suggests that for exploration drawings, as for context drawings, representation does not mean matching some external objects or even some already formed mental image. The drawing does not carry some fixed meaning predetermined at the moment of its inscription; rather, the drawing can be assigned any meaning the designer chooses, either in drawing or interpreting, and the meaning not only can, but must, change. The drawing's meaning must change for the designer to read more out of the drawing than was put into it. Thus exploration drawings embody still another role of representation: inducing change.

The passage from the interview with Eisenman also raises two new points: first, the drawing is a text in the making; and second, drawing and writing are contingent processes whose structure and meaning depend on the uncertain act of making them.

Regarding the first new point: Eisenman and I are talking about the act of making the drawing-as-text. This act of concurrent drawing and interpreting is the essence of the exploration drawing. The exploration drawing as a text, unlike other written or graphic texts, exists only for the moment that the designer makes and interprets it within the working process. Exploration drawings are unique in that only one person's interpretation counts within the working process: the designer's. He or she is the only person whose moment-by-moment interpretation actually gets incorporated into the evolving design task. Only the designer interprets the text of the exploration drawing on the spot, in the act of making it or immediately after, and then, as far as the working process goes, the drawing is either rejected, transformed, or incorporated into some context drawing. Thus the exploration drawing-text acquires whatever meaning the designer gives it in the present moment of the working process, and the meaning assigned by the designer's interpretation of the drawing is special in that it is the one that gets built. If the designer saves the exploration drawing, it may be interpreted as a text by someone else, as I have done repeatedly in this discussion. Its later interpretation by anybody (including the designer), however, is irrelevant to the actual working process and design task that generated it. All subsequent interpretations serve some purpose other than moving the original design project forward.

And regarding the second new point about drawing and writing as contingent processes: the making and interpretation of exploration drawings is similar in some ways to composition and interpretation in language.[10] Both drawing and language have an internal order that influences how their elements relate to each other, but this internal order of the medium cannot be assumed to coincide with an external order of some objective world. Yet the internal order of the medium affects external action. Language's internal rules about subjects and predicates, word order and tenses influence how people think about—and use—space and time, objects and attributes. So also with drawing: as the discussion in chapter 5 showed, drawing's internal rules about graphic conventions and projections influence how designers think about—and design—architectural spaces and objects. Drawing has less extensive and less explicit internal rules than language does, however, so making exploration drawings is inherently more uncertain than writing language, and is more under the subjective influence of the designer.

Thus the exploration drawing, like its written counterpart, is an abstract graphic mark open to interpretation. The drawing is more than just a graphic variation on a graphic theme, however, because it must be capable of changes in meanings; it must be ambiguous enough to induce new interpretations.

Ambiguity in exploration drawings does not imply unskillful drawing; it takes both skill and experience to make and interpret drawings that are productively ambiguous. Exploration drawings may be ambiguous partly because of their graphic characteristics. Kahn's drawing (figure 7-2), for example, is typical of ambiguous drawing with its freehand lines of uneven width and density, its irregular figure, its apparently casual positioning of drawings, and its variable scale relations. Ambiguity does not necessarily require fuzzy lines, however, as Aalto's drawing (figure 7-8) shows: a drawing may be ambiguous partly because the designer simply decides to think of it that way, as described in the discussion about the key graphic/cognitive interactions in chapter 5. The eventual purpose of all study drawings,

---

[10]This is not to say that the order of graphics and written language are the same or even directly correlated. Potential correlations between written language and drawing have been pursued without much success by many authors, including myself (Herbert 1988).

including exploration drawings, is to reduce the ambiguity of the whole design task, to produce a set of construction documents that minimizes the amount of interpretation to be made in the field or the shop.[11] Within the design task, however, the initial statement, or restatement of the exploration drawing from its parent context drawing, must be ambiguous enough to attract, admit, and hold new information from the designer's cognitive experience as the drawing engages the schematization process. Ambiguity is created, or at least allowed, at the inscription of the exploration drawing and then resolved in its transformation.

Closely related to the ambiguity of exploration drawings is their imaginal quality. Study drawings are intrinsically imaginal, so they directly engage the imaginal level of schematization in Rusch's model (figure 5-2). As Rusch points out, the imaginal level lies between the formal and kinesthetic levels, a position that allows the graphic image to engage the designer's larger experience more directly than purely formal concepts can. It would be impossible for design to proceed by using the numeral 3 to signify *Romanesque block capital* in Scarpa's exploration drawing of column capitals, for example, though the image might easily be coded to that symbol for other purposes. The image accounts for the way exploration drawings work (always providing that they are sufficiently ambiguous) and for their central function in architectural design.

Drawings that are ambiguous and imaginal allow the designer to bring new meanings deeply connected to his or her larger experience, including personal as well as architectural associations, back to the context drawing for integration with the current state of the whole design task.

REINTEGRATING EXPLORATION AND CONTEXT DRAWINGS

Returning an exploration drawing to its parent context drawing with its load of new meanings demands new adjustments in both of them. The designer needs to adjust the new information brought by the exploration

drawing to fit the context drawing—to reconnect the ties that were broken through all the structuring operations that abstracted, manipulated, and reformulated the exploration drawing. The designer must also adjust the context drawing to receive the new information brought by the exploration drawing. Such adjustments inevitably affect still other aspects of the context drawing; the returned exploration and its consequent adjustments become new marks in a new context, and thus they start a new cycle of exploration drawings for resolving new design tasks at a next higher level. This relationship of context and exploration drawings is similar to the description by Sergio Los (1984, 164-65) of Scarpa's working process: "A drawing of the whole, indicating the context building. . . . This drawing would remain as the frame of reference throughout the design process, and the solution of specific problems would be transferred to it as they were gradually worked out. . . . By working in this way, Scarpa was able to identify the problems which needed more detailed investigation and which in turn gave rise to further problems, to be similarly translated into drawings."

In this step-by-step fashion the context drawings approach a conclusion to the whole design task, each step becoming a basis for the next step. And, as shown earlier, this stepwise development transcends the immediate design situation: Rusch's model of cognition showed that the creation of new meanings involves the continuous recombination of immediate and remembered experience into new structures, and may include formal, kinesthetic, and emotional as well as imaginal meanings. Here is confirmation of our intuitive sense that design study drawings are the medium in a heuristic process— not just for working through a particular design task, not just for adding to our knowledge of design, but also for understanding the world we live in.

REFERENCES

Derrida, Jacques. 1977. Signature event context. *Glyph* 1:181.

Haber, Ralph, and Maurice Hershenson. 1980. *The Psychology of Visual Perception.* New York: Holt, Rinehart and Winston.

Hatton, Brian. 1988. Fractal geometry. *Building Design* April 1: 2.

---

[11]The reduction of ambiguity applies only to the drawings, not necessarily to the building they describe.

Herbert, Daniel M. 1988. Study drawings in architectural design. *Journal of Architectural Education* 41 (2), Winter: 26-38.

Los, Sergio. 1984. The designs for the central pavilion of the Bienniale. In *Carlo Scarpa, The Complete Works.* Milan: Electa Editrice.

Miller, George A. 1967. The magical number seven plus or minus two: some limits on our capacity for processing information. *The Psychology of Communication.* New York: Basic Books, pp. 14-44.

Nicolis, John S., and Ichiro Tsuda. 1985. Chaotic dynamics of information processing: the 'magic number seven plus-minus two' revisited. *Bulletin of Mathematical Biology* 47 (3): 343-65.

Rusch, Charles W. 1970. Understanding awareness. *Journal of Aesthetic Education* October 4 (4): 57-79.

Stoker, Douglas F., and Nicolas Weingarten. 1983. Computers: CAD vs. CAD. *Architectural Record* December: 20-21.

Ullman, David G., Stephen Wood, and David Craig. 1990. The importance of drawing in the mechanical design process. *Computers and Graphics* 14 (2).

In the introduction I showed how the argument of the book could suggest applications for handmade graphics. Here I will note applications for computer-aided design (CADD)[1] systems. The notes in this appendix are more speculative than the analytic material of the book, and, perhaps, more likely to be overtaken by new developments in the field.[2]

Appendix

NOTES ON APPLICATION FOR COMPUTER-AIDED DESIGN SYSTEMS

FROM HANDMADE DRAWINGS TO CADD SYSTEMS

The body of the book considers issues pertaining to the role of media in design—issues such as *order, representation, transparency, interpretation, ambiguity,* and *uncertainty.* Although these issues and their applications were derived from the analysis of handmade drawings, they can be extended to apply to computer-aided systems.

A diagram will help explain the extension. The properties of handmade drawings may be expressed graphically as an *interface* between the designer and handmade drawings (figure App-1, *left*). Repeating and amplifying the diagram pictures a similar interface between the designer and CADD systems (figure App-1 *right*). The form of the diagram invites extending abstracted concepts from the designer/drawing interface to the designer/CADD interface. Furthermore, the position of the two rectangles suggests a relation between them—a new interface between handmade and CADD systems. This third interface expresses a possibility for integrating features of both systems rather than forcing a choice between them.

With this set of three-way relations in mind I will propose several examples of ways that concepts from handmade drawings could be applied to increase the effectiveness of CADD systems—all, I believe, within the capability of current hardware and software.

---

[1] I will use CADD to mean a computerized system that integrates both design and drafting, although in most cases the discussion focuses on the design functions. I intend CADD also to include what some other writers focusing on computer-aided architectural design have called CAAD.

---

[2] For an earlier version of the relation between study drawings and CADD applications, see Herbert 1987, in end-of-chapter references.

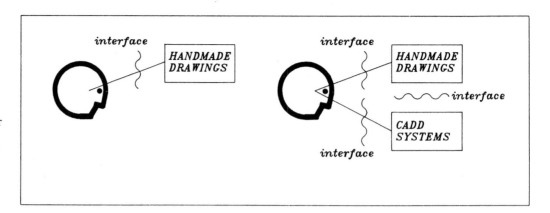

FIGURE App-1. (Left) Interface between designer and handmade drawings. (Right) Interfaces between designer, handmade drawings, and CADD systems. *Courtesy Daniel Herbert.*

MAKING CADD SYSTEMS MORE EFFECTIVE

The following examples illustrate both method and content: the method of extending concepts from handmade drawing to CADD systems and the content of the CADD application. Although some of the functions mentioned in these examples may be available now in CADD systems, the point of the examples is that these functions should be coordinated as parts of an integrated CADD system.

DRAWING/INTERPRETATION AND GRAPHIC AMBIGUITY

The most important way to make current CADD systems more effective concerns the graphic ambiguity of the drawing/interpretation cycle: CADD systems should incorporate an optional mode for ambiguous graphic representation. The foregoing chapters argue that the process of drawing and interpreting ambiguous images is a fundamental characteristic of graphic thinking. In chapter 5, the description of the two key graphic-cognitive interactions asserts that the designer in certain situations must intend a new mark drawn into the visual field to be ambiguous—that is, subject to more than one interpretation so as to permit reading more out of a mark than went into it. In chapter 7, graphic ambiguity is described as partly a matter of the designer's deciding to think of something as ambiguous and partly an attribute of fuzzy, irregular, or uneven lines, and variable scale relations. Graphic ambiguity is a valuable graphic tool, and any medium

that can produce irregular figures can produce graphic ambiguity.

Armed with this information, designers should see a need for graphic ambiguity in certain design situations and they should expect to get it at will from a CADD system. Indeed, CADD systems should provide more and better ambiguity than handmade drawings can. For example, computer displays might introduce ambiguity in irregular overlays of various colors, in shapes and spaces as well as lines, or in images with any specified degree of irregularity. Graphic ambiguity might be produced in time as well as space, through oscillations or progressive movements of the electronic image.

Other research has acknowledged graphic ambiguity as a design issue. William Mitchell (1989a) has suggested that the next phase of CADD research should include concern for computer systems that support ambiguity in shape interpretation, noting that overstructured computer systems tend to impoverish the designer's opportunities to recognize emergent subshapes as new design ideas. Goldman and Zpedski (1988), with a technique called "pixelization," and van Bakergem and Obata (1991), with their "squiggly pen" plotting, have begun to find specific program elements that can produce graphic ambiguity in computer representations.

Thus the concern for ambiguity in CADD systems is not new, but the discussion in the body of the book establishes a new theoretical basis for ambiguity, locates its functions in the working process of design, and allows specification for its incorporation in CADD systems. Graphic ambiguity is so fundamental that I will assume it as included in all of the following examples.

INCREMENTAL REFINEMENTS AND MAJOR REORGANIZATIONS

A next way to make CADD systems more effective has to do with incremental refinements and major reorganizations. Current CADD systems—which typically favor incremental refinements—should provide options that would encourage *found, chosen,* or *forced* reorganizations as described in chapter 5. Here, too, as in the case of ambiguity, CADD systems should go beyond the limitations of pencil and paper media: a dynamic and deliberately fuzzed replay of a series of incremental refinements, for example, might induce major reorganizations that would be impossible with merely static representations. Several of the computer graphic representation techniques described in recent publications (for instance, Zpedski and Goldman 1987) could serve if they were enriched by combination with graphic ambiguity. Other options such as easy zooms, varying degrees or kinds of ambiguity in representations, unorthodox views or impossible projections, figure/ground or color reversals,

color or dynamic overlays could—at the designer's volition or, perhaps, imposed by a random function of the program—jolt the designer's working process out of a sequence of incremental refinements and into a major reorganization.

CONTEXT AND EXPLORATION DRAWINGS

The complementary relation between context and exploration drawings provides another means of making CADD systems more effective: an option in support of exploration drawings. As described in chapter 7, one important way of generating new meanings in design is for the designer to abstract, reformulate, reinterpret, and reintegrate exploration drawings spun off from a parent context drawing. Although typical CADD systems seem well suited to provide the overall function of context drawings, better exploration functions are needed. System options should include ways to make very fast "aside" or overlay sketches separate from the context drawing. One CADD system now under development already has the beginnings of such an exploration option; it provides an electronic equivalent to the sketchpaper overlay and irregular drawing mode (figure App-2).[3]

The analysis of handmade drawings shows that the designer must interact with the drawing. The ability of CADD systems to enlarge an area of a context drawing by zooming is not a substitute for exploration drawings because the electronic operation does not involve the designer's perception, cognition, and action systems in generating new meanings. A subprogram that would make an enlarged (or reduced) copy of a segment of the context drawing might produce the effect of an exploration drawing if the copy were also distorted—say, by being automatically warped and made irregular—so that the designer had to reformulate it in some way before returning its result to the context drawing. The purpose of the exploration drawing is not just to have the drawing appear on the computer screen but to engage the designer in manipulating it.

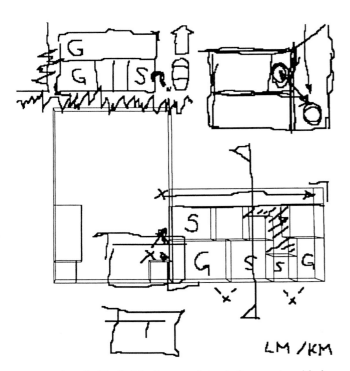

FIGURE App-2. Kevin Matthews: printout of computer-aided drawing showing "freehand" overlay sketching function on a "hardline" cutaway perspective of a floor plan, April 14, 1992. The drawing was made during a 50-minute desk critique in a design studio. *Courtesy Kevin Matthews, Design Integration Laboratory, University of Oregon.*

[3]These functions are part of a proprietary computer-aided system called *Design Workshop* under development by the Design Integration Laboratory at the University of Oregon. The sketch overlay option has been included in the system partly through the influence of material in this appendix.

THE DESIGN WORKPLACE

As a last example, CADD systems should be made more effective by a new approach to the design workplace that supports the integration of electronic and manual systems. The discussion in chapter 7 described how the designer's memory map allows a directed search of a pool of temporary images pinned up around the typical workplace. CADD systems should provide equally direct and uninterrupted access to displays with wide fields of view. Scrolling is not a substitute for a full field of view: the workplace should incorporate head and eye movements that activate the function of the cognitive memory map. Even very fast serial displays across a single monitor do not involve the kinesthetic and perceptual continuity that are essential features of the highly evolved system of human perception and cognition that every designer brings to the design task. Filling a 180-degree-wide by 180-degree-high field of view with video displays is probably neither economically nor psychologically desirable for architectural work stations, however; a mix of electronic and paper graphics seems appropriate. Such a mix could be obtained if the CADD system were to provide for very fast print-outs of screen images onto paper and very fast scanning of paper images or other electronic recordings into the CADD system. Scanned images should be incorporated as objects capable of being manipulated in the working process. Mitchell's (1989b) statement that "specialized input/output devices . . . become very cost-effective when they serve large networks" suggests that rethinking the CADD workplace should include attention to both isolated and networked systems.

These four examples do not exhaust the possibilities for making CADD systems more effective through concepts abstracted from handmade drawings. Other concepts that might be applied to CADD systems include compensating for information losses by deeper, broader, and more flexible methods for storage and access of information; emphasizing imaginal and kinesthetic operations over formal ones; investigating the role of graphic conventions in CADD networks; facilitating the cross-reading of conventions; and increasing drawing speed. Readers will, I hope, find still other applications based on their own experience.

In addition to suggesting applications for increased effectiveness, extending the critical discussion of hand-made drawings raises fundamental questions about the premises of current CADD systems and the directions for their future development.

NEW DIRECTIONS FOR CADD SYSTEMS

And this will be the difficulty. The communication system of the inside world will be highly selective. One will on the whole see only people one intends to see, and since one can scarcely intend to see people of whose existence one is unaware, one will in effect see only people one knows already.

MICHAEL FRAYN, *A Very Private Life*

This quote from Frayn's novel underscores Mitchell's (1989a) warning about overstructured computer systems tending to diminish creative opportunities in design. Such warnings—taken together with the theoretical discussion of critical issues in handmade drawing—suggest new directions for design, research, and development of CADD systems. The examples of these directions given below are inherently speculative; I intend them as invitations for readers to find their own interpretations from the theoretical argument of the foregoing chapters.

UNCERTAINTY AND INTERVENTION

Computer-aided systems should allow for intervention that can open the design task to uncertainty and challenge familiar working processes. As the discussion in chapter 3 showed, our accustomed working processes provide dependability, coherence, and predictability only at the cost of losing touch with any world that does not already conform to our knowledge. Every CADD program—like every handmade graphic system—necessarily includes its own unspoken assumptions about the role of media in design, and as Bruegmann (1990, 144) has pointed out, it also includes a "prehistory, an iconography, and an aesthetic." Thus every CADD program incorporates a tacit order, most of whose elements must be suppressed into a background so that the work can go forward. Following the discussion in chapters 4 and 5, instead of automatically accepting this tacit order, designers using CADD systems should be able to gain access to its suppressed elements, to seek the unpredictable and the unknown, to introduce uncertainty in the design task. Just as for handmade drawings, computer-aided systems should be taken as neither neutral nor transparent: CADD systems, like study drawings, should be engaged as artifacts with their own open structure that can be modified either by chance or by deliberate strategies.

Modifications by chance should include not only the possibilities for graphic accidents, but the means for users to recognize and capture them. These modifications should intervene in the elemental drawing operations such as the mark/interpretation cycle described in chapter 5, because these operations are the generators of design information and so offer especially powerful sites for influencing design outcomes. For modifications by chance, a program might randomly introduce non-Euclidean transformations of the design geometry during design explorations so that the designer would always have to consider other possibilities than the one(s) he or she had intended. For modifications by deliberate strategies, the designer might use graphic algorithms such as Yessios (1987) described for a design studio where design generators were based on fractal geometries, arabesque ornamentations, and diagrammatical representations of biological processes.

TRANSPARENCY AND OTHER MEDIA

The challenge to transparency in CADD systems must go beyond allowing users to set operating parameters; just as for handmade graphics, designers using CADD need to be able to make basic changes in the medium. Scanning photographic images into architectural drawings, for example, has already made a good start toward breaking open CADD systems from their drawing-only mode. Engaging non-architectural databases in art history, cinema, advertising, and photojournalism should follow (who except Tigerman, for example, would put Dachau into an architectural database?). Yet even these extensions of present CADD systems would be limited by their need for translation into the operating and display systems of the computer and would thus invite the user to regard them as transparent. Intervention should be able to open the electronic structure itself.

Opening the electronic structure could incorporate not just the scanned images but the actual operations of other disciplines: theater, dance, music, painting, sculpture, and—as Yessios and Eisenman have shown—science. Computer-aided systems could participate in a network of multi-media working processes for design. Such a role would make CADD media always a foreground issue—no more transparent in the working process than programmatic and site issues are now.

DESIGNING DESIGN SYSTEMS

Efforts to make computer-aided design systems more open and to connect them with other open systems would inevitably reflect uncertainties into the processes for designing the systems themselves. In this reflexive situation, the subject of the design process—the CADD system—would necessarily take on the characteristic uncertainties of the process it is intended to facilitate—the design working process. For example, feeding the issues of ambiguity and uncertainty back into the process of designing the CADD system suggests that programs for producing graphic ambiguity in CADD systems might themselves be ambiguous, and that the source of random geometric transformations might not be a program of specified transformations but an indeterminate connection to some other open system.

Thus (at a more general level) the designers of CADD systems are not allowed to be meta-designers. Their medium is neither neutral nor transparent; it is just as problematic as that of architectural designers. From this perspective, the CADD system ceases to be a stable system at all; the designing of the CADD system, the CADD system, the architectural design task, the construction industry, the built environment, and its users all form a complex of interacting and competing—and often incoherent and contradictory—foreground issues.

As chapter 3 has shown, design in the past has had to thrust all but a few issues into the background because that has been the only way we, as designers using a limited working process based on handmade drawing, could get on with the work; we have had to assume an essentially closed and stable design system. Over the past 20 years, research and development of CADD systems have sought to replace this closed and stable handmade system with a new but also essentially closed and stable electronic system. Designers of the new electronic systems have rejected the handmade aspect of the previous system but have kept—or, perhaps, have codified and reinforced—its closure and stability. Each CADD system is based on some stable version of an architectural design process. As each stage of research and development reaches closure, the system is updated and published as a new coherent edition (e.g., Upfront 1.1, Archtrion II 5.51b) whose properties and processes are stable, if not always predictable.

New CADD systems should not be designed for closure and stability, however, but for openness, instability, and uncertainty; rather than call for more rigorous and closed orderings of the design process, their designers should search for new, open kinds of order in such fields as fractals and chaos theory to which only computers can provide access. These systems should be conceived as systems-in-becoming, whose properties become manifest only at some particular moment of use. To paraphrase Stanley Fish's description of interpretation from chapter 4, a CADD system ought to be a *moving field of concerns, at once wholly present (not waiting for intention but constituting intention) and continually in the act of reconstituting itself.*

REFERENCES

Bruegmann, Robert. 1989. The pencil and the electronic sketchboard: architectural representation and the computer. In *Architecture and Its Image,* ed. Eve Blau and Edward Kaufman, pp. 139-55. Montreal: The Canadian Center for Architecture.

Goldman, Glenn, and M. Stephen Zpedski. 1988. Abstraction and representation: computer graphics and architectural design. In *Computing and Design Education; Proceedings of the 1988 Workshop of the Association for Computer Aided Design in Architecture,* ed. Pamela J. Bancroft, pp. 205-16.

Herbert, Daniel M. 1987. Study drawings in architectural design: applications for CAD systems. In *Integrating Computers into the Architectural Curriculum; Proceedings of the 1987 Workshop of the Association for Computer Aided Design in Architecture,* ed. Barbara-Jo Novitski, pp. 157-68.

Mitchell, William J. 1989a. A new agenda for computer aided architectural design. In *New Ideas and Directions for the 1990s; Proceedings of the 1989 Workshop of the Association for Computer Aided Design in Architecture,* ed. Chris I. Yessios, pp. 27-43.

———. 1989b. Panel discussion no. 1: CAAD systems of the 90s. *1989 Workshop of the Association for Computer Aided Design in Architecture.* In *ACADIA Newsletter* 8(5): 21.

van Bakergem, W. Davis, and Gen Obata. 1991. Free hand plotting. St. Louis: Urban Research and Design Center, Washington University.

Yessios, Chris I. 1987. A fractal studio. In *Integrating Computers into the Architectural Curriculum; Proceedings of the 1987 Workshop of the Association for Computer Aided Design in Architecture,* ed. Barbara-Jo Novitski, pp. 169-81.

Zpedski, Stephen, and Glenn Goldman. 1987. Form, color and movement. In *Integrating Computers into the Architectural Curriculum; Proceedings of the 1987 Workshop of the Association for Computer Aided Design in Architecture,* ed. Barbara-Jo Novitski, pp. 39-50.

Alexander, Christopher, Sara Ishikawa, and Murray Silverstein. 1977. *A Pattern Language: Towns, Buildings, Construction.* New York: Oxford University Press.

Arnheim, Rudolph. 1969. *Visual Thinking.* Berkeley: University of California Press.

Baxandall, Michael. 1972. *Painting and Experience in Fifteenth Century Italy,* New York: Oxford University Press.

Broadbent, Geoffrey, Robert Bunt, and Charles Jencks, ed. 1980. *Signs, Symbols and Architecture.* Chichester: John Wiley and Sons, Inc.

Bruegmann, Robert. 1989. The pencil and the electronic sketchboard: architectural representation and the computer. In *Architecture and Its Image,* ed. Eve Blau and Edward Kaufman, pp. 139-55. Montreal: The Canadian Center for Architecture.

Bucher, François. 1968. Design in Gothic architecture, a preliminary assessment. *Journal of the Society of Architectural Historians* 27 (March): 49-71.

Bunn, James, H. 1981. *The Dimensionality of Signs, Tools and Models.* Bloomington: Indiana University Press.

Carroll, David. 1987. *Paraesthetics.* New York: Methuen.

Chastel, Andre. 1961. *The Genius of Leonardo da Vinci.* New York: The Orion Press.

Crowe, Norman, and Steven Hurtt. 1986. The acquisition of architectural knowledge. *Journal of Architectural Education* 39(3).

Davis, Michael T. 1983. 'Troys portaulx et deux grosses tours': the flamboyant facade project for the cathedral of Clermont. *Gesta* 22 (1): 67-80.

De Franclieu, Françoise. 1981. *The Le Corbusier Sketchbooks,* ed. Françoise De Franclieu, vol. 2. New York: Architectural History Foundation; Cambridge: MIT Press.

Derrida, Jacques. 1977. Signature event context. *Glyph* 1:181.

Dreyfus, Hubert, and Paul Rabinow. 1983. *Michel Foucault, Beyond Structuralism and Hermeneutics.* Chicago: University of Chicago Press.

Eco, Umberto. 1976. *A Theory of Semiotics.* Bloomington: Indiana University Press.

———. 1980. Function and sign: the semiotics of architecture. In *Signs, Symbols and Architecture,* ed. Geoffrey Broadbent, Richard Bunt, Charles Jencks, pp. 33-67. Chichester: John Wiley and Sons, Inc.

Eisenman, Peter, 1988. Architecture as a second language: the texts of between. *Threshold: Journal of*

BIBLIOGRAPHY

the School of Architecture, University of Illinois at Chicago 4 (Spring): 71-5.

———. 1989. Blue line text. In *Deconstruction/Omnibus Volume,* ed. A. Papadakis, C. Cooke, A. Benjamin, pp. 150-51. New York: Rizzoli International Publications, Inc.

———. 1989. Eisenman builds. *Progressive Architecture* (October): 67-99.

———. 1989. En terror firma: in trails of grotextes. In *Deconstruction/Omnibus Volume,* ed. A. Papadakis, C. Cooke, A. Benjamin, pp. 152-53. New York: Rizzoli International Publications, Inc.

Empson, William. 1963. *Seven Types of Ambiguity.* London: Chatto and Windus.

Fish, Stanley. 1980. *Is There a Text in This Class?* Cambridge, Mass.: Harvard College Press.

Foucault, Michel. 1970. *The Order of Things.* New York: Random House.

Gadamer, Hans-Georg. 1976. *Philosophical Hermeneutics.* Berkeley: University of California Press.

Goldman, Glenn, and M. Stephen Zpedski. 1988. Abstraction and representation: computer graphics and architectural design. In *Computing and Design Education; Proceedings of the 1988 Workshop of the Association for Computer Aided Design in Architecture,* ed. Pamela J. Bancroft, pp. 205-16.

Gombrich, E.H. 1960. *Art and Illusion.* New York: Pantheon.

Goodman, Nelson. 1968. *Languages of Art.* New York: Bobbs-Merrill Company, Inc.

Haber, Ralph, and Maurice Hershenson. 1980. *The Psychology of Visual Perception.* New York: Holt, Rinehart and Winston.

Harvey, John. 1950. *The Gothic World.* London: B.T. Batsford, Ltd.

———. 1972. *The Mediaeval Architect.* New York: St. Martin's Press, Inc.

Hatton, Brian. 1988. Fractal geometry. *Building Design,* April 1: 2.

Hawkes, Terence. 1977. *Structuralism and Semiotics.* Berkeley: University of California Press.

Herbert, Daniel M. 1987. Study drawings in architectural design: applications for CAD systems. In *Integrating Computers into the Architectural Curriculum; Proceedings of the 1987 Workshop of the Association for Computer Aided Design in Architecture,* ed. Barbara-Jo Novitski, pp. 157-68.

———. 1988. Study drawings in architectural design. *Journal of Architectural Education* 41(2, Winter): 26-38.

———. 1992. A media course in architectural study drawings. In *American Institute of Architects Architectural Education Programs Monograph, 1991 Education Honors,* pp. 37-42.

Hewitt, Mark A. 1985. Representational forms and modes of conception. *Journal of Architectural Education* 39(2): 2-9.

Jurgens, Hartmut, Heinz-Otto Peitgen, and Dietmar Saupe. 1990. The language of fractals. *Scientific American* (August): 60-67.

Laseau, Paul. 1986. *Graphic Thinking for Architects and Designers,* 2d ed. New York: Van Nostrand Reinhold.

Le Corbusier. 1957. *The Chapel at Ronchamp.* New York: Frederick A. Praeger.

———. 1960. *My Work.* London: The Architectural Press.

———. 1982. *The Le Corbusier Archive.* Vol. 20, *Ronchamp, Maisons Jaoul, and Other Buildings and Projects.* New York: Garland Publishers; Paris: Fondation Le Corbusier.

Lockard, William Kirby. 1982. *Design Drawing.* Tucson, Ariz.: Pepper Publishing.

Los, Sergio. 1984. The designs for the central pavilion of the Bienniale. In *Carlo Scarpa, The Complete Works.* Milan: Electa Editrice.

Lyndon, Donald. 1982. Design: inquiry and implication. *Journal of Architectural Education* 25(3, Spring): 2-8.

McKim, Robert H. 1980. *Thinking Visually.* Belmont, Calif.: Wadsworth, Inc.; Lifetime Learning Publications.

McMahon, A.P. 1956. *Leonardo da Vinci, Treatise on Painting.* Princeton, N.J.: Princeton University Press.

Miller, George A. 1967. The magical number seven plus or minus two: some limits on our capacity for processing information. In *The Psychology of Communication,* pp. 14-44. New York: Basic Books.

Mitchell, William J. 1989. A new agenda for computer aided architectural design. In *New Ideas and Directions for the 1990s; Proceedings of the 1989 Workshop of the Association for Computer Aided Design in Architecture,* ed. Chris I. Yessios, pp. 27-43.

———. 1989. The death of drawing. *UCLA Architecture Journal* (2): 64-69.

Nicolis, John S., and Ichiro Tsuda. 1985. Chaotic dynamics of information processing: the 'magic number seven plus-minus two' revisited. *Bulletin of Mathematical Biology* 47(3): 343-65.

Norberg-Schulz, Christian. 1975. *Meaning in Western Architecture.* New York: Praeger Publishers.

Novitski, Barbara-Jo. 1991. CADD holdouts. *Architecture* (August): 97-99.

Papadakis, A., C. Cooke, and A. Benjamin, ed. 1989. *Deconstruction/Omnibus Volume.* New York: Rizzoli International Publications, Inc.

Pauly, Daniele. 1980. *Ronchamp, Lecture d'une Architecture.* Paris: A.P.P.U.; Ophrys.

———. 1982. The Chapel of Ronchamp as an example of Le Corbusier's creative process. *The Le Corbusier Archive.* In Vol. 20, *Ronchamp, Maisons Jaoul, and Other Buildings and Projects,* pp. ix-xix. New York: Garland Publishers; Paris: Fondation Le Corbusier.

Porter, Tom. 1979. *How Architects Visualize.* London: Studio Vista.

Reidmeister, Andreas. 1982. The sketch as a practical instrument. *Daidolos* (September): 26-34.

Ricoeur, Paul. 1981. *Hermeneutics and the Human Sciences.* Cambridge: Press Syndicate of the University of Cambridge.

Rusch, Charles W. 1969. On the use of leveling and sharpening as an analytic tool in the study of artistic behavior. In *Proceedings, 77th Annual Convention.* American Psychological Association. Pp. 478-79.

———. 1970. Understanding awareness. *Journal of Aesthetic Education* 4(4 October): 57-79.

Saint-Martin, Fernande. 1990. *Semiotics of Visual Language.* Bloomington: Indiana University Press.

Scarpa, Carlo. 1984. *The Complete Works.* Milan: Electa Editrice.

Seung, T.K. 1982. *Structuralism and Hermeneutics.* New York: Columbia University Press.

Stent, Gunther. 1978. *Paradoxes of Progress.* San Francisco: W. H. Freeman and Company.

Stiny, George Nicholas. 1985. Computing with form and meaning in architecture. *Journal of Architectural Education* 39(1): 7-19.

Stoker, Douglas F., and Nicholas Weingarten. 1983. Computers: CAD vs. CAD. *Architectural Record* (December): 20-21.

Thoenes, Christof. 1982. St. Peter's: first sketches. *Daidolos* (September): 81-98.

Tschumi, Bernard. 1989. Parc de la Villette, Paris. In *Deconstruction/Omnibus Volume,* ed. A. Papadakis, C. Cooke, A. Benjamin, pp. 175-81. New York: Rizzoli International Publications, Inc.

Ullman, David G. (publication pending) A model of the mechanical design process based on empirical data. *Journal of Artificial Intelligence for Engineering Design, Analysis and Manufacturing.*

Ullman, David G., Stephen Wood, and David Craig. 1990. The importance of drawing in the mechanical design process. *Computers and Graphics* 14 (2).

van Bakergem, W. Davis, and Gen Obata. 1991. Free hand plotting. St. Louis: Urban Research and Design Center, Washington University.

White, Edward T. 1983. *Site Analysis.* Tucson, Ariz.: Architectural Media Ltd.

———. 1986. *Space Adjacency Analysis.* Tucson, Ariz.: Architectural Media Ltd.

Whiting, Cecile. 1989. *Antifascism in American Art.* New Haven, Conn.: Yale University Press.

Yessios, Chris I. 1987. A fractal studio. In *Integrating Computers into the Architectural Curriculum; Proceedings of the 1987 Workshop of the Association for Computer Aided Design in Architecture,* ed. Barbara-Jo Novitski, pp. 169-81.

Zpedski, Stephen, and Glenn Goldman. 1987. Form, color and movement. In *Integrating Computers into the Architectural Curriculum; Proceedings of the 1987 Workshop of the Association for Computer Aided Design in Architecture,* ed. Barbara-Jo Novitski, pp. 39-50.

INDEX